# SUPER·TOYS

# SUPER·TOYS

## Penny Warner

St. Martin's Press
New York

Design by Laura Hough

Library of Congress Cataloging in Publication Data

Warner, Penny.
    Super toys.

    1. Toy making.   I. Title.
TT174.W37   1985          745.592          84-23800
ISBN 0-312-77657-8
ISBN 0-312-77658-6 (pbk.)

First Edition
10 9 8 7 6 5 4 3 2 1

*To my husband, Tom, who magically turned trash into toys. And to my children, Matthew and Rebecca, who happily put them to the test.*

# Acknowledgments

My sincere thanks to the many parents and professionals who contributed in some way to *Super Toys:* Constance Pike from Chico State University, Marcy Libster from the Jewish Community Center, Anne Arns and Joanne Dahlin from the Danville Coop, Barbara Pedersen from the Rainbow Coop, Barbara Swec from the Italian Women's Club, Dr. Eileen Jackson and Dr. Arthurlene Towner from the Special Education Department at San Francisco State University, the Family Life Department staff at Diablo Valley College, the San Francisco Switchboard, the Nurture Company and Parent-Infant Education of Contra Costa County, Chris Saunders, Lucy Galen, Mary and Ralph Warner, Melanie Thiele, and Geoffrey and Edward Pike.

I would also like to thank all the kids who gave *Super Toys* their durability tests: Holly Kralj and Simonie Thiele, Tim and Jana Swec, Kristin and Brooke Saunders, Jondrea (J.R.) Rile, Keri Dickerson, Jason Cosetti, David Ashley, and Lucy, John, and Joseph Simpson.

And a very special thanks to Gloria Safier, my agent, and Barbara Anderson, my editor.

# Contents

# Introduction

With the price of toys today, who can afford to fill the toy box anymore? You can! With the help of *Super Toys*.

*Super Toys* is a collection of ideas I have presented over the years on three San Francisco–based television talk shows, "People Are Talking," "A.M. San Francisco," and "T.G.I.4."

I have received thousands of requests for information and instructions, and now realize that there are a lot of parents, grandparents, relatives, and friends out there who want to create quality playthings for children.

Today's parents are interested not only in providing creative toys for their children, but also in making the toys themselves—provided, of course, they don't take a great deal of time and money to make, and don't turn into trash as soon as they're completed.

Super Toys are fast and easy to make. The instructions are written clearly, with precise illustrations to ensure success.

Super Toys are economical. It's frustrating to pay a lot of money for a toy that barely lasts until bedtime. Most of the toys in *Super Toys* are made from discarded or household items—the cost is practically nil!

Super Toys are safe. You know your child's developmental level and play ability better than anyone else, and you can remedy every potential hazard to ensure your child's safety.

Super Toys are quality toys. Adding your creative, personal touch makes each toy unique and special.

Super Toys are learning materials. Each toy is an open-ended, stimulating plaything that can be adapted and used by children of any age. And each offers your child one or more skills to encourage optimum learning.

The book provides a wide range of toys: soft toys to cuddle, bath toys for water play, flying toys for space exploration, and so on. There are ten chapters, each dealing with a different type of toy.

Super Toys provide a great way to express your love and affection for your child. What a joy it will be to see his or her face when you present your latest creation!

It's time to start filling the toy box . . . with Super Toys!

# How to Use This Book

*1. Start collecting! Find a large cardboard box to hold collectibles and toss them in as you come across them. Here are some valuable items: cardboard tubes, scraps of paper, yarn, string, fabric remnants, ribbons, straws, toothpicks, Popsicle sticks, jars, lids, plastic containers, egg cartons, paper cups, clothespins, milk cartons, and squirt bottles.*

*2. Put together a basic toy-making kit consisting of: scissors, stapler, needle and thread, crayons, paint, washable and permanent felt-tip pens, clear Con-Tact paper, tagboard (cereal boxes make good tagboard), cardboard, and glue.*

*3. Make the toys together. They were designed to be created by child and parent side by side.*

*4. Add decals, detail, and decorations to your toy to make it look its best. If you paint it, consider using varnish and/or clear Con-Tact paper to enhance longevity.*

# For Safety's Sake

*1. Do not use any bottle that contained harsh chemicals, bathroom disinfectant, ammonia, or any other harmful substance.*

*2. Use lead-free enamel paint.*

*3. Use white, nontoxic glue (such as Elmer's) unless otherwise directed.*

*4. For young children, sew on details and facial features securely whenever possible, instead of gluing.*

*5. Match the toy to your child's developmental level or adapt the toy to suit his or her ability.*

*6. Check for sharp edges, breakable parts, loose, swallowable pieces, and so on.*

*7. Nontoxic felt-tip pens are water soluable. "Permanents" are not and should be used under adult supervision.*

# · 1 ·

# *Bath Toys*

The bath procedure around our house was always the same. As soon as I called "Bathtime!" our calm and happy home instantly turned into a scene right out of a grade-B horror movie. While I ran around the house looking for my dirt-encrusted children, they scattered to the ends of the place, hiding from the dreaded Bath Monster. When I finally discovered them, I had to drag them bodily down the hall to the bathroom. Their filthy nails grabbed for every doorjamb. Their screams were piercing: "I just had a bath last week!"

Bathtime got to be such a hassle I found myself dreading it more and more each time. But when I realized my dog smelled sweeter than my children, I knew I had to do something to make bathtime more inviting. The following toys proved to be the most popular lures into the bath water. So grab the shampoo—it's bathtime!

# Spongies

◆

## Materials

*Scissors*
*Old sponges (all different colors and
    sizes)*
*Broad-tipped permanent felt-tip pen*

This is an easy project that can make
the bath water a sea full of fantasy amphib-
ians. Cut old sponges of different colors
and sizes into animal shapes, using the
scissors. Outline the edges with permanent felt-tip pen and add detail to the
faces.

You might also try some other shapes.
Cut out alphabet letters, geometric
shapes, flowers, or create your own
shapes. And here's a trick: Place the
sponge shapes on the tile wall of the bath
and press the water out—they'll stick!

# Thunderstorm

◆

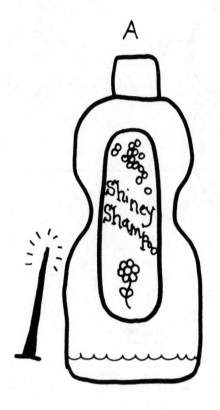

A

## Materials

*Plastic bottle (shampoo, dishwashing liquid, etc.)*
*Metal skewer (or other sharp instrument)*

You can create an indoor rainstorm with this simple-to-make toy. Thoroughly clean plastic bottle *(A); do not use* any bottle that contained harsh chemicals, bathroom disinfectant, ammonia, or any other harmful substance. Pierce *one* side with skewer to make holes *(B)*.

Fill with tub water and raise above head, holey side up. Turn over and squeeze *(C)!*

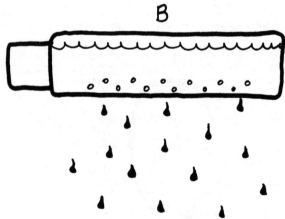

B

C

# Wuppet

◆

## Materials

*Scissors*
*1 hand towel (or 2 washcloths)*
*Permanent felt-tip pen (or colored thread for sewing machine or embroidery floss and needle)*
*Pompon (about 1 inch in size, available at fabric or hobby stores)*

Is it a puppet? Is it a Muppet? No! It's a wet, washable wuppet—and a great way to get clean behind those dirty ears.

Using the pattern shown on pages 6–7 (A), cut out animal shapes from hand towel folded in half or from 2 washcloths (B). Draw a face with permanent felt-tip pen or sew on eyes, mouth, whiskers, and so on with a fancy machine stitch or by hand with embroidery floss and needle; add pompon for nose (C). Make sure all additions are sewn on securely. With right sides together, seam sides, leaving bottom edge open for the child's hand (D). Turn right side out. Fold up cuff (to hold soap, etc.) and topstitch around outside edge of puppet (E).

Now run a bath and start the "Wuppet Show."

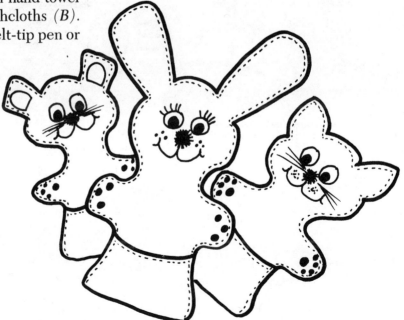

A

pompom nose

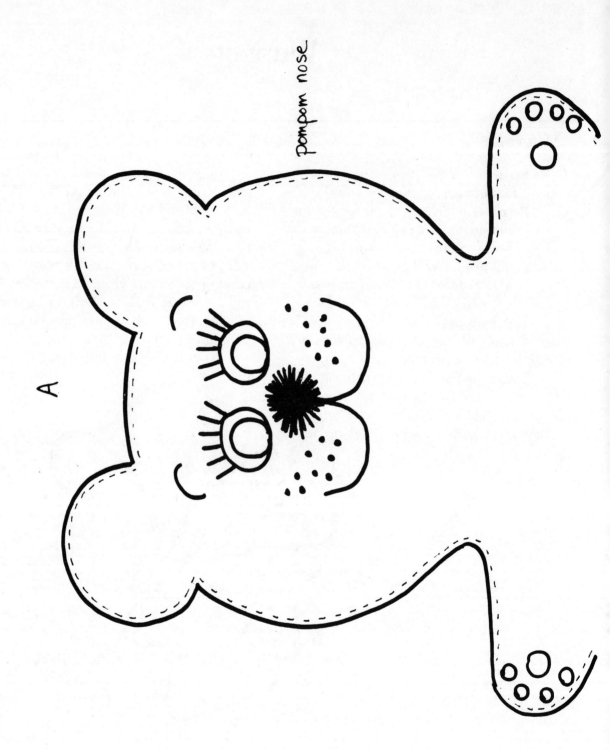

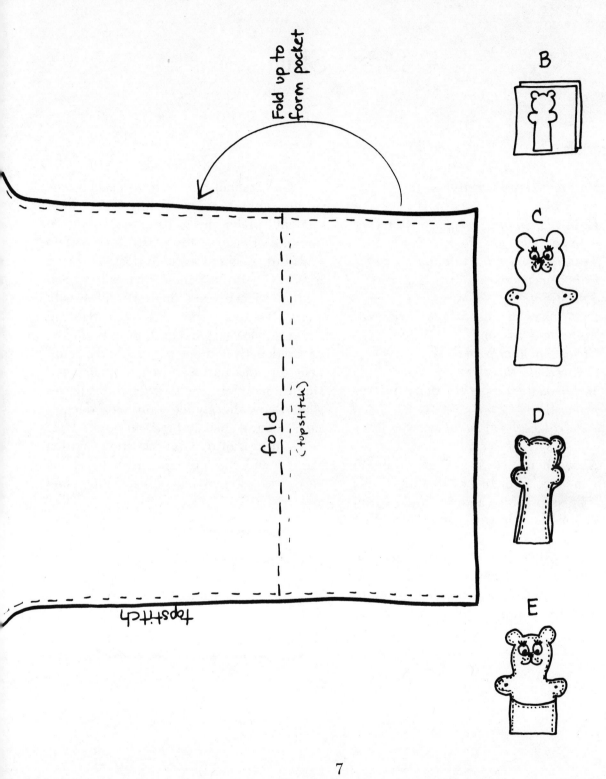

Fold up to form pocket

fold
(topstitch)

topstitch

B

C

D

E

# Pirate Ship

◆

## Materials

*Half-gallon milk carton*
*Scissors*
*12-inch strip of wood-grain Con-Tact paper*
*2 plastic margarine-tub lids*
*Rubber cement*
*3 plastic straws*
*Small piece of colorful fabric (or second milk carton)*
*Clear Con-Tact paper*
*Colored plastic tape*
*Metal skewer (or other sharp instrument)*
*2 short lengths of yarn*

Ahoy there, ye swabs! It's time to scrub the deck—er, neck. But first, let's build the ship. Rinse and dry milk carton and cover it with wood-grain Con-Tact paper. As shown in (A), use scissors to make a cut, 1 inch from bottom, through one side of carton and extending 1 inch down the sides. Make a slit at the top. Fold in sides and top to make deck (B).

Cut 3 small circles from each plastic lid and glue to sides of ship with rubber cement. Make three 1-inch-long cuts in one end of each of the plastic straws; fold ends out. Cement ends to deck as shown in (C). Cut three 3-inch squares from colorful fabric covered on both sides with clear Con-Tact paper. (You can also cut these squares from another milk carton covered with contact paper.) Make a slit near top and bottom of each square and slip them over the straws; the squares should bow slightly like sails. Add decorations, using plastic-tape cutouts. Poke holes in tops of two outside straws with a skewer and in ends of carton to attach yarn, as shown in illustration. Sail away. . . .

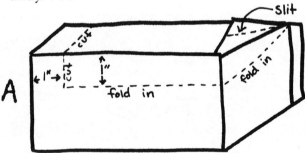

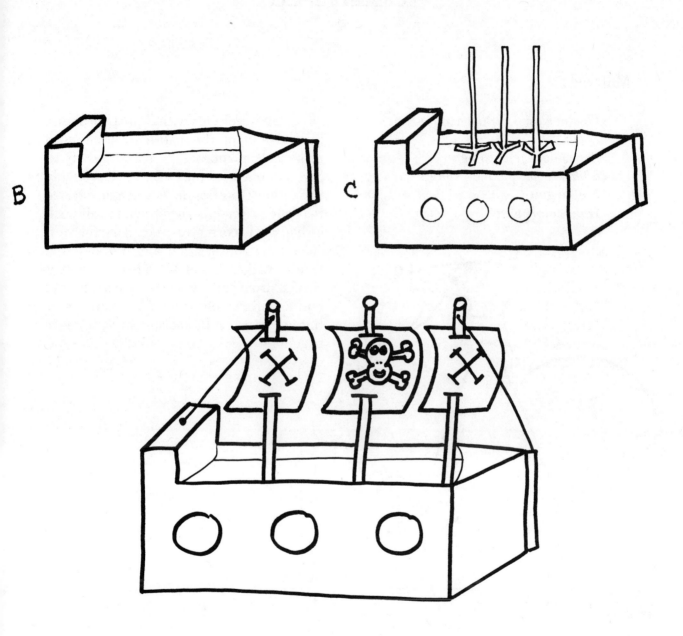

B     C

# Squirt Bird

◆

## Materials

*Plastic squirt bottle (window cleaner, etc.)*
*Permanent felt-tip pen*
*2 plastic margarine-tub lids*
*Staple gun*
*Food coloring*

Play water war with Squirt Bird, and by the end of the battle everyone will make a clean getaway.

To make Squirt Bird, thoroughly rinse squirt bottle; *do not use* any bottle that once contained harsh chemicals such as lye, acid, corrosives, etc. Dry the outside of the bottle. Draw a bird face on the handle with permanent felt-tip pen. Cut "wings" from tub lids and staple to sides of bottle with staple gun. Fill with water tinted with food coloring and squeeze trigger.

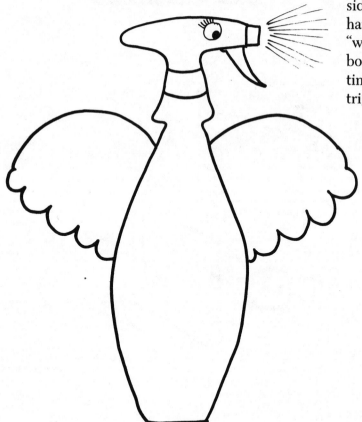

# · 2 ·

# *Soft Toys*

How would you like to have a doll that looks exactly like you? Or a hand puppet representing characters from a favorite storybook?

These and the other Soft Toys in this chapter do not require expert sewing ability, and they can be made primarily from leftover fabrics and yarn. Soft toys stimulate imagination, provide hours of creative play, and give comfort. They are ideal to use with the Storybook Theater described in Chapter 5, and don't forget to bring them along on those long trips to Grandmother's house to fill the backseat hours with fantasy and fun.

# Pompon Power

◆

## Materials

*Scissors*
*2 pieces corrugated cardboard (each
    at least 1 foot square)*
*Bright-colored yarn (½ skein of 2 col-
    ors or ⅓ skein of 3 colors)*
*Full-length pencil (or stick of similar
    size)*
*X-acto knife (or other sharp knife)*
*Dental floss (or strong nylon thread)*

You can make this colorful and fun toy in one evening, while you watch your favorite television programs.

Using the pattern shown on page 13 *(A)*, cut 2 circles from the cardboard. Place the circles together. Wrap yarn from one skein around full length of pencil until you have a "cigar" about the size of the hole in the cardboard, as shown on page 14 *(B)*. Cut yarn, wrap it around cardboard doughnut, passing pencil around and through hole *(C)* and wrapping all the way around circle until it is one solid color. Then change to a new color *(D)*. Repeat with second color, then third, until you can *no longer* fit the yarn through the hole. Be sure you keep yarn taut but not tight *(E)*.

When hole is filled, cut yarn along edge of cardboard with X-acto knife *(F)*, being careful not to pull apart any yarn. After cutting completely around the cardboard, slip a piece of dental floss or strong nylon thread between the pieces of cardboard to the center and tie *tightly (G)*. Cut off cardboard and gently remove from yarn *(H)*. Fluff the ball and trim any rough edges.

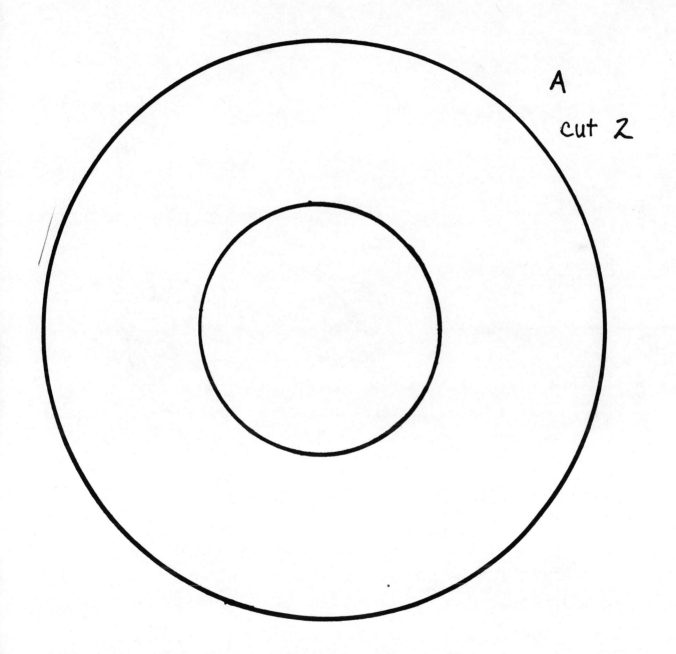

A

cut 2

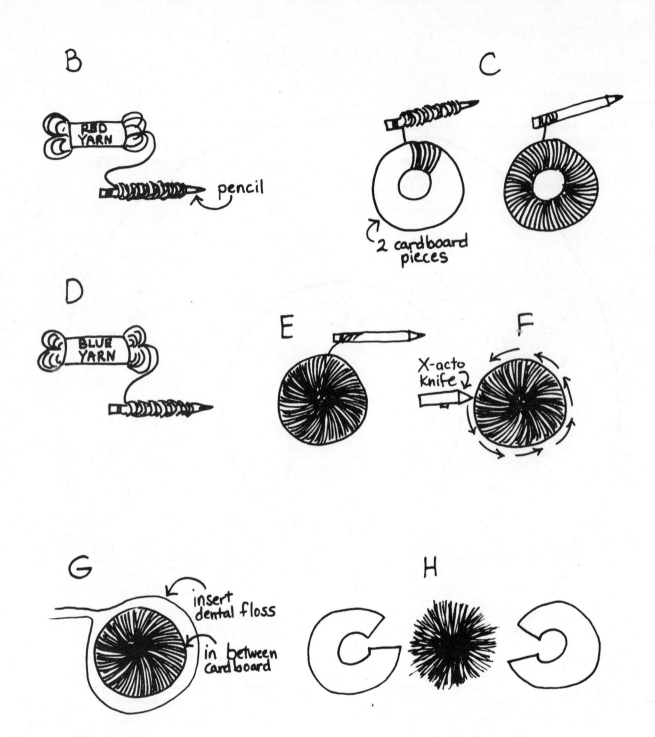

B

RED
YARN

pencil

C

2 cardboard
pieces

D

BLUE
YARN

E

F

X-acto
knife

G

insert
dental floss

in between
cardboard

H

14

# Gotcha! Glove

◆

## Materials

*1 old glove*
*Scissors*
*Yarn remnants*
*Needle and thread*
*2 small pompons (available at fabric
    or hobby store)*
*White glue (such as Elmer's)*
*2 plastic eyes (available at hobby
    store)*

This makes a great "I'm gonna getcha"
tickle hand.

Make sure the old glove is clean. Cut
bunches of yarn into 5-inch lengths. Lay
one bunch on top of glove and sew in
place; lay another bunch in a different di-
rection and sew in place. Repeat until yarn
completely covers glove; be careful not to
sew glove shut. When all the yarn is secure, tack pompons on securely for eyes.
Glue a plastic eye in center of each pompon and allow to dry. (If your child is
under two, omit plastic eyes.) Slip glove
on and find someone to tickle.

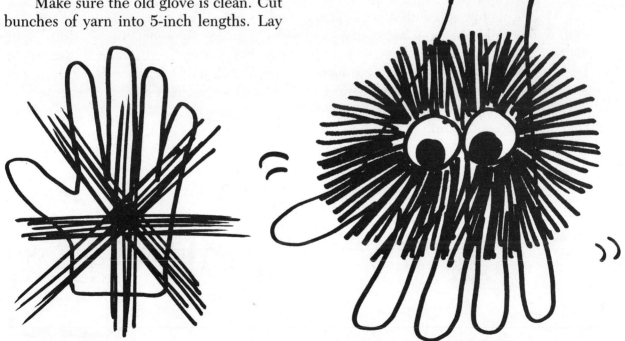

# "Me" Doll

◆

## Materials

*Photograph of child (a good head shot)*
*1 yard solid-color polyester fabric (to match skin color of child)*
*Scissors*
*Sewing machine (or needle and thread)*
*Polyester fiberfill (or fabric scraps or old pantyhose) for stuffing*
*Permanent felt-tip pens (or acrylic paints), a variety of colors*

Here's a little doll with a familiar face.

Find a photograph with a good head shot of your child (A) and have it enlarged (B) to 5-x-7-inch size at the photo store. Take the photo to a T-shirt shop and have them make it into a transfer. (Be sure to call ahead to see if they offer this service.) Fold the polyester fabric in half and cut the piece in two along the fold. When you return to pick up the transfer, bring along one of the pieces and have the transfer put near the top of the shorter edge of the fabric (C).

At home, draw a doll body, to fit size of head, on a piece of paper to use as a pattern; be sure to allow for a ¼-inch seam allowance, and don't make the arms and legs too thin or you'll have trouble turning the doll right side out. Cut out 2 pieces of fabric, one that incorporates the transfer, and place right sides together (D). Sew edges together, leaving a 3-inch opening at one side to allow for stuffing. Turn right side out and stuff with fiberfill. Sew seam opening closed by hand. Add clothing detail with permanent felt-tip pens or acrylic paints. (Be careful not to stick any pins in it. . . !)

C

cut 2

D
right sides together

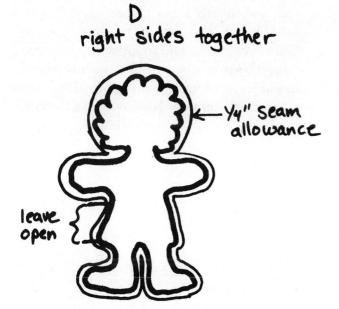

¼" seam
allowance

leave
open

17

# Old MacDonald's Farm

◆

## Materials

*1 garden glove*
*White glue (such as Elmer's)*
*Needle and thread (optional)*
*5 small, closely clipped pompons (2 pinks, 1 yellow, 1 brown, 1 white; available at fabric or hobby store)*
*Scissors*
*Scraps of colored felt*
*1 yellow feather*
*1 small farmer hat (available at hobby store)*
*10 small plastic eyes (available at hobby store)*
*Permanent felt-tip pen*

Here's an idea for making traveling more fun. This farmer puppet should provide hours of backseat play.

(You can use the same method for other puppets. If you need ideas, dig out some children's books. You'll find ideas for making The Three Little Pigs, Peter Pan and friends, or Snow White and the Four Dwarfs—ran out of fingers!)

Find a single garden glove and run it through the wash, if necessary. To make Old MacDonald's Farm, glue or sew pompons—the 2 pinks for the farmer and the pig, the yellow for the chick, the brown for the cow, and the white for the sheep—onto glove fingers as shown, and allow to dry. Cut ears, noses, beaks, cow horns, and bowtie from felt. Glue ears, horns, feather, hat, and bowtie to glove fingers. Glue eyes, nose, and mouths to pompons. Glue the cow's eyes to felt horns. Write the animal sounds on the glove with permanent felt-tip pen. Now, how's your singing voice?

# Mini-Monsters

◆

## Materials

*Scissors*
*1 old knitted glove, fingers intact*
*Needle and thread*
*10 tiny buttons or beads*
*Scraps of yarn*
*Scraps of felt*

Cut fingers off glove. To the fingers, sew tiny buttons or beads for eyes and nose. Use pieces of yarn and felt to add hair, ears, tails, and so on, and sew them on puppets. Slip finished puppets onto your fingers and make up a story.

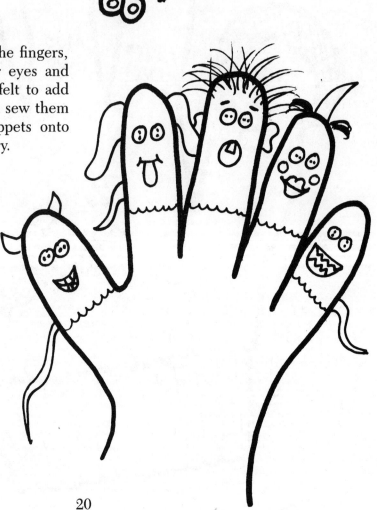

# Finster Fishbone

◆

## Materials

*1 sock with toes (or a regular sock)*
*Polyester fiberfill (or pieces of scrap fabric or old pantyhose) for stuffing*
*Scissors*
*2 pieces (3 inches each) of yarn*
*Needle and thread*
*Scraps of felt*
*White glue, such as Elmer's (optional)*

This silly fish will swim into a little one's heart. A sock with toes works best for this soft toy, but you can adapt a regular sock, too.

Stuff toe sock (A) with fiberfill. If you're using a regular sock, make a seam about 1½ inches from toe end. Cut end into fringe, then stuff rest of sock with fiberfill. After sock is stuffed, tie a piece of yarn about one-fourth of the way down from the toes to make tail fin (B). To make mouth, tie off 1 inch from end (C). Fold ends back to create "bun" shape for mouth; whipstitch in place. Cut eyes and fins from felt and sew or glue to body.

# Dinosaur

◆

## Materials

*Scissors*
*1 old glove, cleaned if necessary*
*1 square of felt (12 inches on a side)*
*Needle and thread*
*3 buttons (or felt) for eyes and nose*
*Felt-tip pen*

The preschool/kindergarten child is particularly attracted to dinosaurs, and it's especially exciting to have one that comes alive.

Cut old glove up the back almost to tip of middle finger *(A)*. Cut out spine from felt, using pattern *(B)*. Turn glove inside out and insert spine into slit. Sew closed so that spine sticks out when glove is turned right side out. Turn glove right side out and sew on button or felt eyes and nose. Draw on mouth with felt-tip pen. Put on glove and make dinosaur "walk" with fingers.

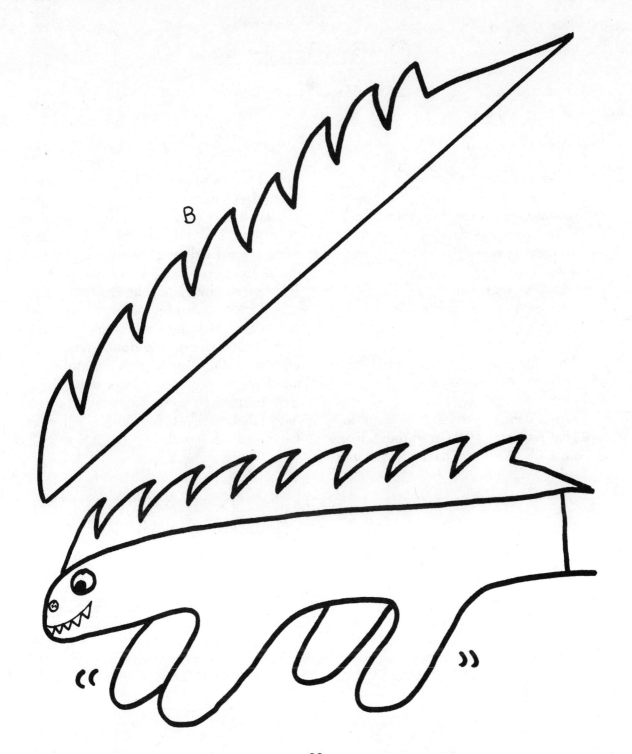

23

# Oscar Octopuss

◆

## Materials

*1 skein of yarn*
*Scissors*
*1 small rubber (or Styrofoam) ball, 2*
*    to 3 inches in diameter*
*Ribbon (optional)*
*2 buttons (or felt) for eyes*
*Needle and thread*
*White glue (such as Elmer's)*
*Scrap of felt*

For this wiggly animal you'll need only two main items—yarn and a small ball *(A)*.

Open skein of yarn and lay it out in a long, flat rectangle *(B)*. Cut through loops at both ends. Now you have a lot of individual pieces of yarn *(C)*. Set one piece of yarn aside; divide remaining yarn in half and lay halves crosswise in the shape of an X, placing ball in center of X *(D)*; gather yarn around ball so it is completely covered. Tie yarn closed under ball with the loose piece of yarn *(E)*; tie tightly.

Divide ends of yarn into 8 even sections *(F)*. Take one section and divide it into thirds for braiding. Braid yarn and tie off end with a small piece of ribbon or another piece of yarn. Repeat until you have braided all 8 sections. Sew 2 buttons onto head for eyes, or glue on felt eyes. Glue on a felt mouth.

A

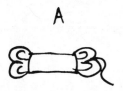

B

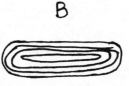

C.

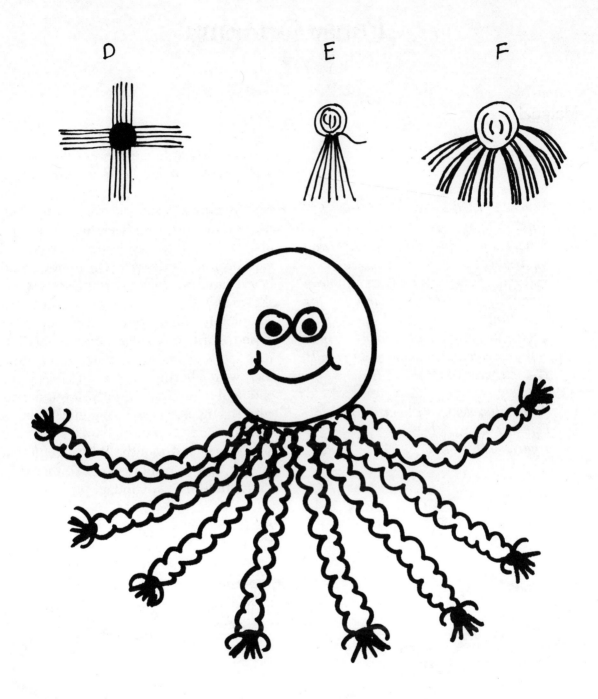

D  E  F

25

# Pansy the Pony

◆

## Materials

*1 large sock*
*Scissors*
*Lengths of scrap yarn*
*1 piece of cardboard (4 × 6 inches)*
*Pins*
*Sewing machine (or needle and thread)*
*Polyester fiberfill (or pieces of scrap fabric or old pantyhose) for stuffing*
*1 long, smooth wooden dowel (1 inch in diameter, as long as child is tall)*
*12-inch piece of strong cord*
*Staple gun*
*White glue, such as Elmer's (optional)*
*Felt scraps*
*1 yard satin ribbon*

The stick horse never goes out of style, and provides lots of imagination play.

Scrounge a soft old sock from Dad's drawer and cut it up back just over curve of heel (A). Turn inside out. Wrap some yarn around cardboard (B); remove cardboard carefully. Pin yarn in place at slit, as shown (C). Repeat this process until slit is completely lined with yarn. Sew slit closed, turn sock right side out, and cut yarn loops to make fringe for mane. Stuff sock with fiberfill. Insert stick into open end and close end tightly around stick with strong cord; use staple gun to secure sock to wood. Sew or glue on felt for eyes, nose, ears, and mouth. With needle and thread, tack colorful ribbon to either sides of mouth for reins. Giddap!

### A      B      C

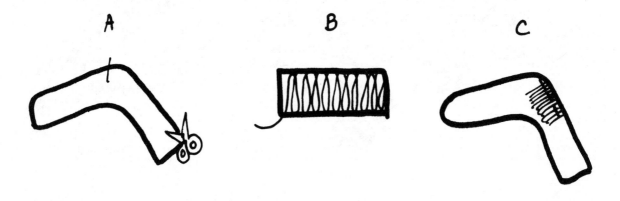

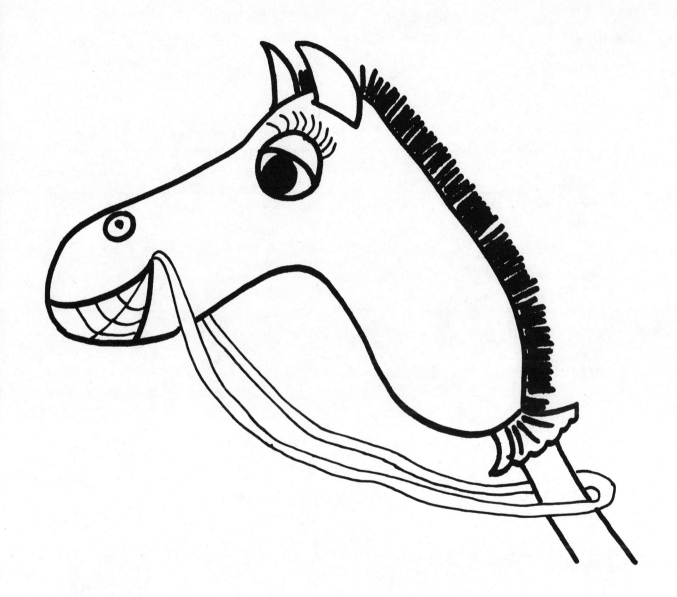

# Magnetic Monsters

◆

## Materials

Scissors
Scrap felt in a variety of colors
White glue (such as Elmer's)
Pompons in several different colors
   (available at hobby store)
Small plastic eyes (available at hobby
   store)
1 roll of magnetic tape (available at
   hobby store)

These hideous monsters can be played with on any metal surface that attracts magnets—great for the refrigerator!

Make up some frightful pompon critters, or use the samples below, by cutting out felt for background, then gluing on pompons, preferably the same color as the background. Glue on eyes, then cut out and glue on arms and legs, mouths, and/or whatever strikes your monster fancy. Cut off a small piece of magnetic tape for each monster and stick to back of felt. Attack the fridge!

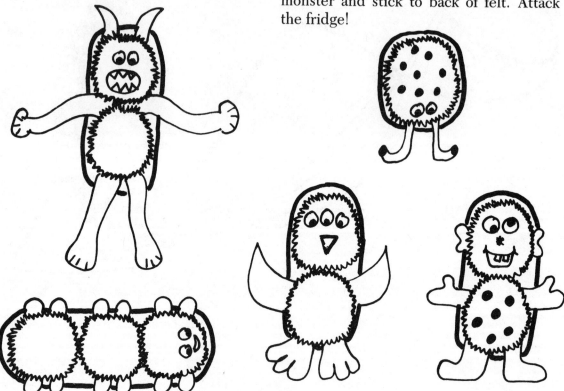

28

# · 3 ·

# *Flying Toys*

What is it about Flying Toys that is so fascinating? The spontaneity? The unpredictability? I don't think it matters. It's fun!

My husband and son made their first flying machine together last year—a homemade kite. They enjoyed working together on the project, and when the masterpiece was completed, we all hiked down to the local "green" for the launch.

It was lovely to see: father and son lying on the grass, watching their artwork soar above the neighborhood while discussing such topics as the future of Little League and the need for increased allowance. It was a great opportunity for them just to spend some time together, and provided lots more than just a few moments of flight.

# Power Plane

◆

## Materials

*2 large Styrofoam meat trays*
*Scissors*
*X-acto knife (or other sharp knife)*
*Enamel spray paint (preferably gold or silver)*
*Plastic tape in different colors (or decals, permanent felt-tip pens, or acrylic paints)*
*1 large paper clip (or 2 small ones)*

Save some Styrofoam meat trays, clean them thoroughly, and turn them into a squadron of 747s.

Using pattern (A), cut out airplane body, wing, and tail from Styrofoam. Using knife, make slits in body as shown, and insert wing and tail (B). Spray with enamel paint (gold and silver look more realistic) and let dry. Add plastic tape cutouts or decals for detail, or use felt-tip pens or acrylic paints (C). Attach paper clip (D) to nose of plane, and, as they say in Houston, we have lift-off!

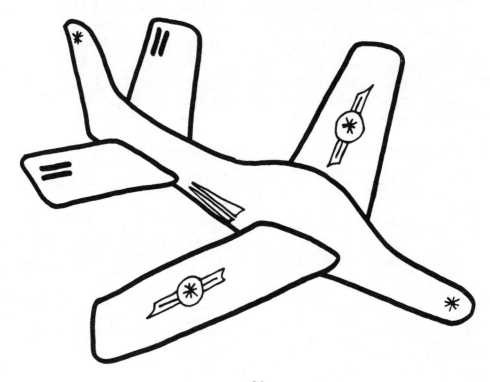

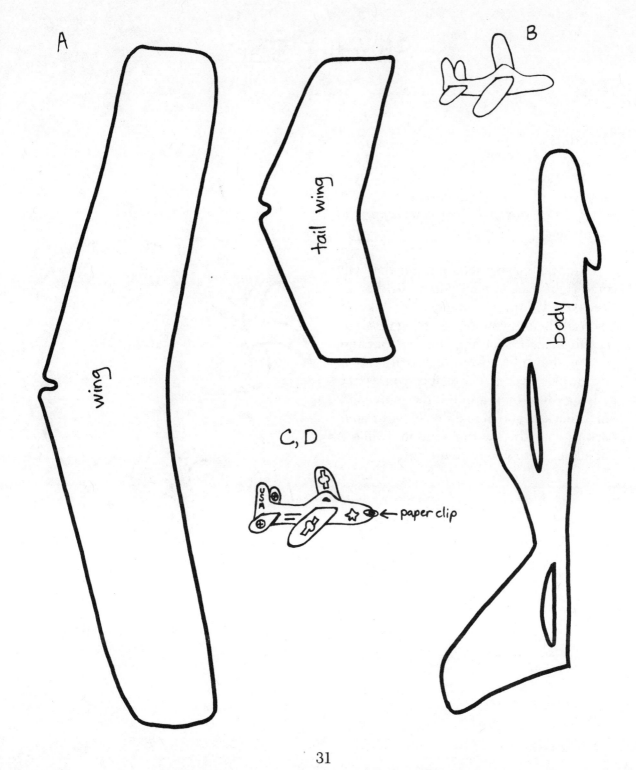

A

wing

tail wing

B

body

C, D

← paper clip

# Shooting Star

◆

## Materials

*Scissors*
*Piece of heavy tagboard (or side of cereal box or balsa wood), approximately 1 foot square*

You can make a shooting star that will come right back to you, with a little practice. And I do mean practice—it takes a few trials before you get the hang of it.

To make a shooting star, cut out the pattern shown *(A)*, from tagboard, cereal box, or balsa wood. Throw it as you would a flying disk (*not* around the porcelain knickknacks), and hopefully it will come back to you *(B)*. Try throwing it at different angles until you have it right.

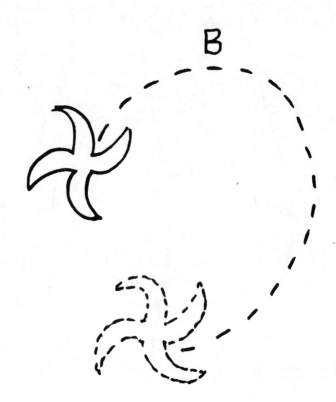

B

33

# UFOs

◆

It is fun and easy to make your own kite, especially if you're working with someone else, and with some imagination you can have the most colorful and creative UFO in the sky.

## Kite Frames

The frame for your kite can be made from either wood or plastic. Wood or bamboo dowels will work, as will plastic rods that may be found at a plastics store or hardware store. The dowels should be about ¼ inch in diameter and, if they are wood, should be soaked in water for a few hours to allow for more flexibility. You'll need 2 dowels for the common kite—30 inches and 24 inches.

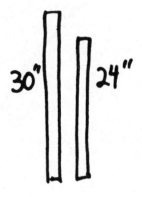

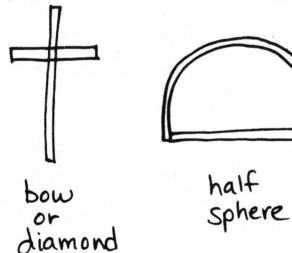

bow
or
diamond

half
sphere

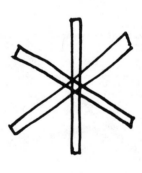

hexagon

## Kite Coverings

There are a multitude of papers and fabrics you can use to construct your kite. Just keep in mind that you want it to be strong yet lightweight. Make sure you have a large enough piece before you begin cutting, although you can seam pieces together if necessary. Here are some suggestions for kite coverings:

*Old sheets*
*Fabric remnants*
*Newspaper comics*
*Brown package wrap*
*Christmas paper or other gift wrap*
*Plastic garbage bags*
*Cellophane*
*Tissue paper*
*Department-store bags—paper or plastic*
*Crepe paper*
*Lining material*
*Mylar (or other plastic) sold by the yard—Mylar is interesting because it is shiny and reflective*
*"Ripstop" fabric (available at most fabric stores for approximately three dollars per yard)—it is virtually indestructible*

## Kite Decorations

Half the fun is decorating your kite before you launch it. You may draw, paint, or glue on decorations, but don't overload it with excess weight or flight ability will be impeded. Here are some materials for decorating:

*Felt-tip pens*
*Watercolors*
*Crayons*
*Poster paints*
*Construction-paper cutouts*
*Posters*
*Tie-dyed fabric*
*Glitter, sequins, stickers, trim, rick-rack, etc.*
*Fringe (for along the edges)*

What to draw:

*Superheroes*
*Geometric designs*
*Flowers, hearts, rainbows, clouds, birds, planes*
*Monsters, dragons*
*Names, messages*
*People, faces, animals*

Be sure to make big, bold, bright designs, filling in with lots of color, so you can see the artwork from a distance.

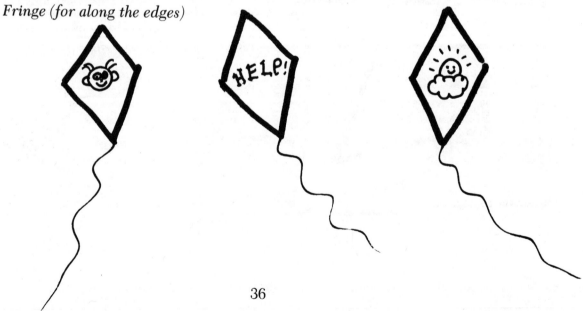

36

## Kite Tails

A kite will spin if it doesn't have a tail. The tail keeps it balanced and upright. It is important to remember that the purpose of the tail is to provide wind resistance, not weight. The friction of the wind blowing over the tail helps to keep the kite upright. The following are suggestions for tails:

*Ribbons*
*Rosettes*
*Paper cups*
*Fabric swatches*
*Tissue paper*
*Paper fans*
*Construction-paper designs*

You can attach the tail with staples, safety pins, paper clips, tape, small rings, or by sewing it on. Make sure the tail is at least 6 times the width of the kite. Most mistakes are made by trying to use a tail that is not long enough for the kite. It's better to have the tail too long than too short.

37

# Diamond Kite

◆

## Materials

*X-acto knife (or other sharp knife)*
*1 wooden dowel (¼ inch in diameter, 30 inches long)*
*1 wooden dowel (¼ inch in diameter, 24 inches long)*
*Ruler*
*String—at least 3 yards*
*White glue (such as Elmer's) or cement*
*Tape (preferably reinforced "post office" tape)*
*Kite string*
*Scissors*
*Kite covering (30 × 24 inches)*
*Needle and thread or staple gun (optional)*
*Kite tail*

You're ready to begin making your kite. We'll start with the most common kite, the diamond kite. It's the easiest to assemble and, for some reason, the most popular, although aerodynamically it doesn't fly as well as some of the others in this chapter.

Carve a V notch at each end of both your wooden dowels. Measure from one end along the 30-inch dowel and mark off 8 inches. Measure from one end along the 24-inch dowel and mark off 12 inches (*A*). Now cross the pieces at right angles to form a cross at the 2 marks; tie the dowels together there with string (*B*). Add some glue for strength and let it dry completely. (You can also tape the dowels together, in which case you should use the glue before applying the tape.) Run a piece of kite string through the notches around the outside of the dowels to form a frame (*C*). Tape around ends to keep string secure. Measure and cut kite covering, allowing a seam margin 2 inches larger than the frame. Lay covering over frame, fold seam allowance around dowels, and glue, sew, tape, or staple closed.

Poke 2 holes diagonally in center of kite, as shown (*D*). Thread a short piece of string loosely through holes and around cross made by the dowels to form a loop. Attach your kite string to this loop and you are ready to fly, as soon as you have added the tail.

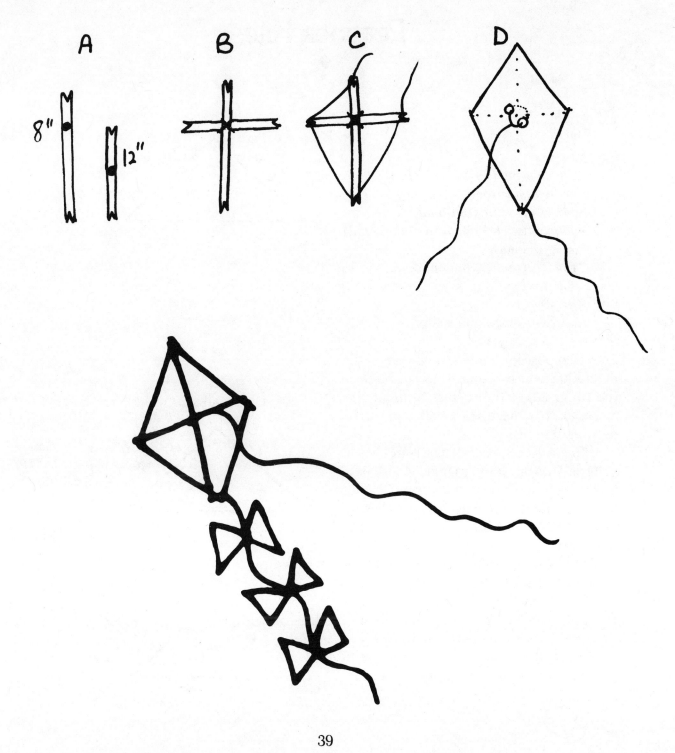

# Peacock Kite

◆

## Materials

*Scissors*
*Kite covering (39 × 19 inches)*
*Needle and thread*
*Sewing machine (optional)*
*2 dowels (each ¼ inch in diameter, 21
   inches long)*
*2 dowels (each ¼ inch in diameter, 18
   inches long)*
*Kite string*
*Nontoxic felt-tip pens*

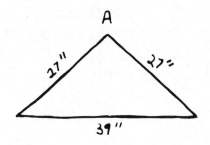

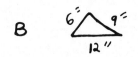

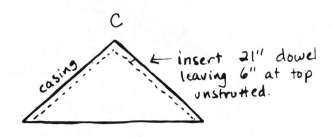

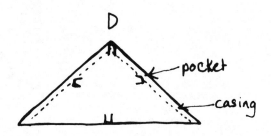

The peacock kite is made from the delta kite, which requires no tail because the wings adjust themselves in flight. It's an easy kite to make, flies well, and can be decorated in many ways.

To make the peacock, cut your chosen material into one large triangle whose base is 39 inches and whose sides are 27 inches long *(A)*. Cut another smaller triangle with sides of 12 inches, 9 inches, and 6 inches *(B)*.

Fold over both 27-inch sides of larger triangle and sew a seam casing 21 inches long and ½ inch wide, 6 inches from tip, for sliding in the two longer dowels *(C)*. Be sure to leave the top 6 inches unstrutted and sew across top of casing to prevent dowels from slipping. Check to make sure dowels fit, then remove them before proceeding to next step.

Cut out four 1-inch square "pockets" from leftover piece of your kite material. Cross and place 18-inch dowels on back of kite to determine pocket placement. As shown in (D), sew these squares using zigzag stitch on underside of kite, one on each side and top and bottom, to create small pockets that open toward center of kite. Sew smaller triangle to right side of larger triangle so that the midpoint of the 12-inch side is at the point where the 2 shorter dowels will meet. Insert the 2 shorter dowels into pockets and tie them at center with string. Slip the longer dowels into seam and sew ends closed (E). Make a small hole at the tip of the smaller triangle with scissors and reinforce with zigzag stitch. Attach your kite string to it (F). Using felt-tip pens, decorate kite with a peacock face and feathers, then watch the peacock fly—an anatomical impossibility!

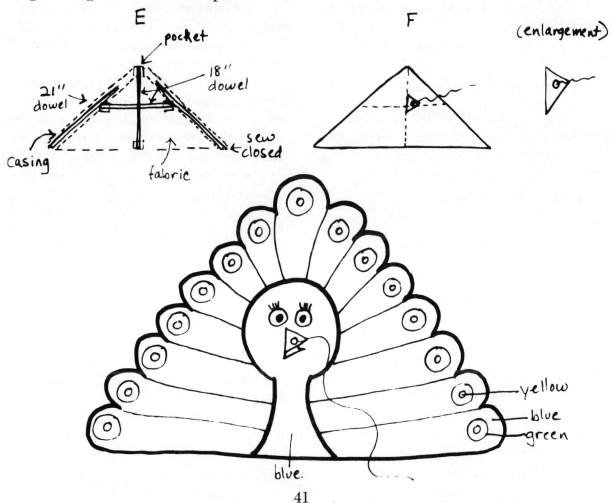

41

# Rainbow Kite

◆

## Materials

*Scissors*

*Material for kite covering (two 36-x-24-inch pieces)*

*Needle and thread*

*Sewing machine (optional)*

*1 dowel (¼ inch in diameter, 48 inches long)*

*1 dowel (¼ inch in diameter, 34 inches long)*

*2 dowels (each ¼ inch in diameter, 22 inches long)*

*Stapler (optional)*

*Acrylic paints (or fabric for appliqués) in rainbow colors*

*6 yard-long streamers or ribbons in rainbow colors*

*Kite string*

This Tiffany-like kite glows in the sky, enchanting everyone who sees it. It's based on the half-sphere kite.

If you have wooden dowels, soak 48-inch one an hour so it can be curved.

Cut 2 half circles from the kite material, 36 inches at the base by 24 inches high *(A)*, and, right sides together, sew them together on the curved edge leaving base open *(B)*. Save the scraps of material. Turn right sides out and sew a ½-inch seam all the way around the curve to make a casing for the dowel *(C)* starting 1 inch up from bottom on left side. Turn edges of base to inside and sew closed close to fold, leaving open a 1-inch slit at left side so that long curved dowel and bottom dowel can be inserted. Sew a casing for bottom dowel as you did for curve *(C)*, making sure you keep the left side open.

Cut out four 1-inch square "pockets" from a leftover piece of your kite material. Cross and place 22-inch dowels on back of kite to determine pocket placement. As shown in *(D)*, sew squares on underside of kite using zigzag stitch, one on each side and one each at top and bottom, to create small pockets that open toward center of kite, being sure to leave casing open. Cut out a 3-inch triangle from leftover kite material and sew, using zigzag stitch, to the front of the kite to create a "bridle," as shown in *(E)*. Cut a small hole in center of small triangle and reinforce with thread. Sew or staple on streamers or ribbons for tail.

Insert 48-inch dowel into curved casing and sew openings closed. Insert 34-inch dowel in base casing and sew openings closed. Insert the two 22-inch dowels into pockets and tie them at center with string *(F)*.

Paint or appliqué a rainbow design on front of kite, as shown on page 44. Attach kite string to bridle and hoist your rainbow skyward.

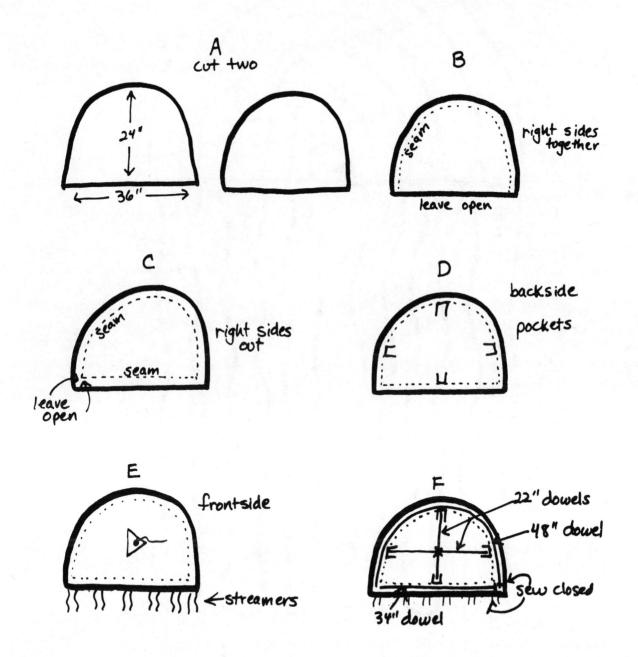

A
cut two
24"
36"

B
seam
right sides together
leave open

C
seam
seam
right sides out
leave open

D
backside
pockets

E
frontside
streamers

F
22" dowels
48" dowel
sew closed
34" dowel

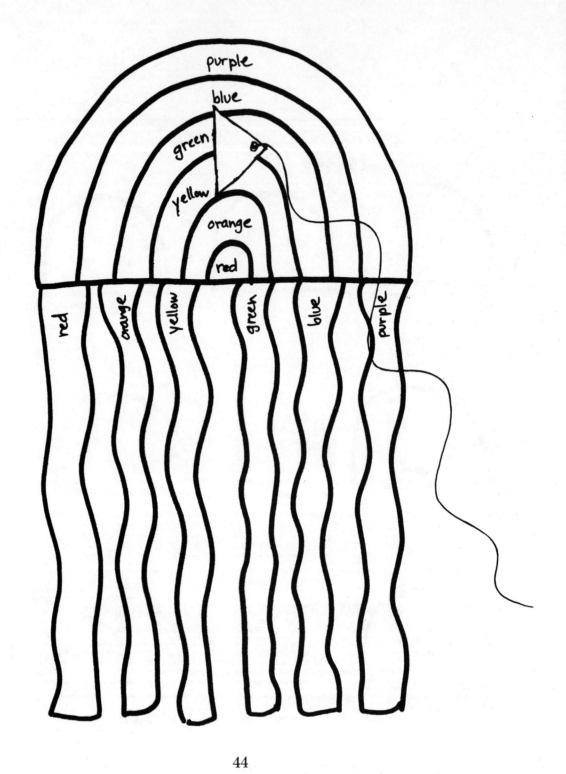

# Mount St. Helens Kite

◆

## Materials

*Same as Peacock Kite (page 40)*
*plus*
*1 bright red yard-long streamer*

This "mountain" kite looks stunning, high in the air, and is easy to create using the delta shape. Follow the instructions for the Peacock Kite to make the delta kite frame. Color your covering to resemble a mountain, like the example shown. Add a bright red streamer at the top to make it look like an erupting volcano, then let it climb.

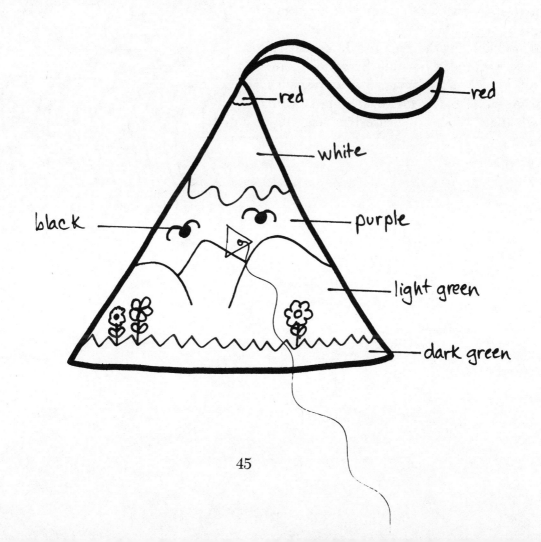

red

red

white

black

purple

light green

dark green

# Dragon Kite

◆

## Materials

*Same as Rainbow Kite (page 42), but using red, black, yellow, and green acrylic paints (or fabric for appliqués) and 6 green yard-long streamers or ribbons*

The Dragon Kite looks frightening up in the sky, with its mean red eyes and sharp teeth. Make the half-sphere kite frame following the Rainbow Kite instructions. Outline a horrible dragon face on your kite covering and color in with shades of green. Tip the green streamers with red, then watch him scare the neighborhood.

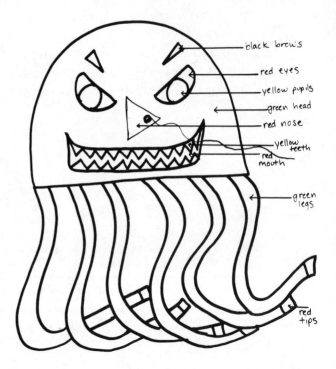

black brows
red eyes
yellow pupils
green head
red nose
yellow teeth
red mouth
green legs
red tips

# Octopus Kite

◆

## Materials

*Same as Rainbow Kite (page 42), but using green and black acrylic paints, white and red construction paper, and 8 green yard-long streamers*

A tentacled octopus is an easy kite to make, and adds a bit of whimsy to the sky. Make the half-sphere kite frame following the Rainbow Kite instructions and paint the covering green. Cut out large white eyes from construction paper and color the pupils black. Add a red construction paper mouth and green streamers for tentacles. Then set him sailing in the clouds.

# Mother Hen and Chicks Kite

◆

## Materials

*Scissors*
*2 pieces material for kite covering (one 36-inch square, one 18-inch square)*
*Poster paint or felt-tip pens*
*Needle and thread*
*3 dowels (each ¼ inch in diameter, 36 inches long)*
*Tape (optional)*
*Kite string*
*8 small paper plates*
*Stapler (or white glue, such as El-mer's)*

If you have a favorite animal, you can adapt this kite to suit. The baby chicks make up the tail, and look so sweet following their mother around in the sky.

Cut out a circle from larger piece of kite material and decorate it like a hen. From the leftover fabric, cut six 1-inch square "pockets." Stitch the pockets on 3 sides at evenly spaced points on the wrong side of the fabric as shown in *(A)*, with openings toward center. Insert dowels and tape or tie together as shown. Make a small triangular bridle, 3 inches on each side, and attach to front *(B)*. Attach string. Color and paint small paper plates to make baby chicks or eggs. Attach with stapler, tape, or glue to tail string, and attach string to Mother Hen at the bottom. Then set them free.

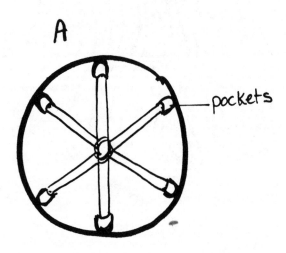

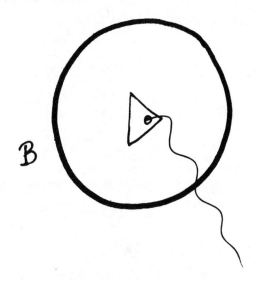

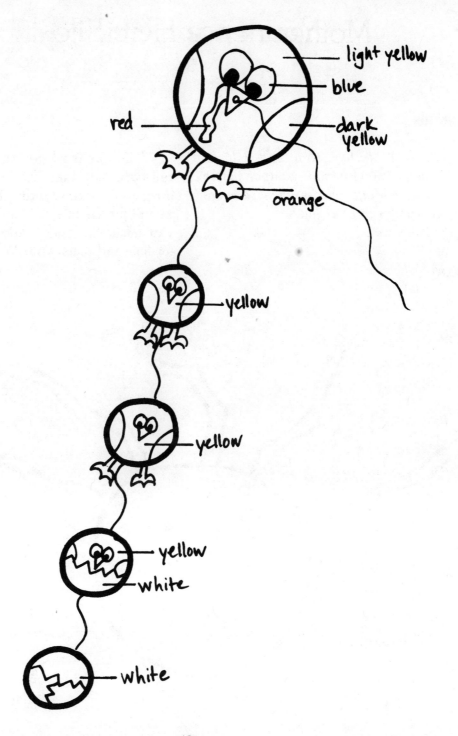

light yellow

blue

red

dark yellow

orange

yellow

yellow

yellow

white

white

# Your-Face-Here Kite

◆

## Materials

*Same as Mother Hen and Chicks (page 48), eliminating paper plates and adding yard-long streamers the color of your hair*

The circular kite frame is ideal for a self-portrait. Make the kite following the directions for the Mother Hen and Chicks, except for the tail. Decorate your covering with a face like yours. Add some streamers for hair and teach your kite to fly!

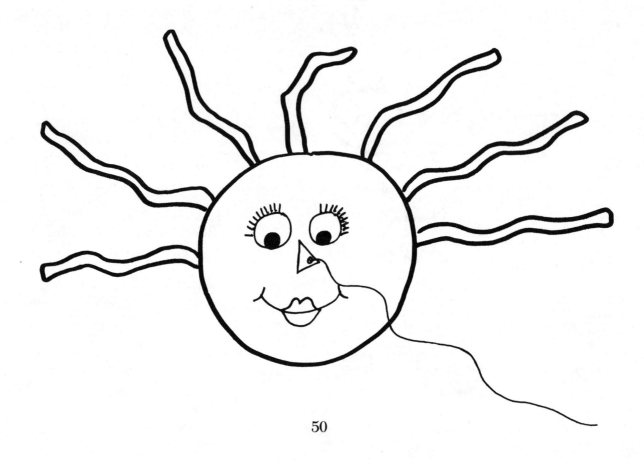

# Go Fly a Kite

◆

Your kite will never get off the ground if you don't know a little bit about aerodynamics. On your first attempt, don't go out in a hurricane thinking the more wind the better. A light wind is best until you become an old pro at kite flying. For safety reasons, avoid areas where there are trees, wires, buildings, and roads. And don't fly your kite in bad weather. An airborne kite attracts lightning, in which case your kite line acts as a conductor of electricity. The result—you could receive a fatal jolt.

Tie the end of your ball of kite string to your kite bridle. Hold the string loosely in your hands or insert a stick through the string skein and let the string unravel as the kite lifts.

Hold the kite with the wind behind you, and let the string out evenly and rapidly. "Winch" launch it—that is, tug the string and let it out. If you feel the kite begin to fall, tug the string again and the kite should soar.

You can add a messenger to your kite string for added fun. Just make a cone shape out of construction paper, or borrow an old pinwheel from the toy chest and add it to the kite-flying string—the wind will pull it up along the string. You might even try a parachute. Make a fabric chute with some small weights attached to the ends of the gathered strings. Tie the top of the chute to the flying string with a slip knot. The wind will take it up, and with a tug on the string you can "eject" it and send it on its way back to earth.

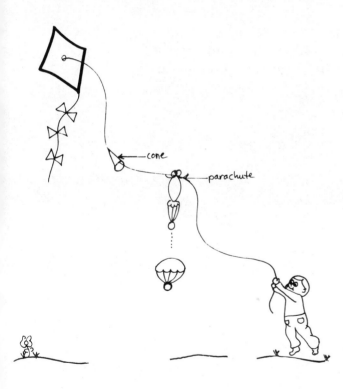

cone

parachute

# · 4 ·

# *Cars and Trucks*

You'll have your own used-car lot with these transportation toys made from empty, discarded household items. You can use some of the cars, trucks, trains, and planes with the Your Town toy from Chapter 6 for added fun.

Be sure to add your personal touch with paint, colored plastic tape, auto decals, stickers, stripping, reflector tape, and glitter to make them the most exciting set of wheels or wings on the block.

# Box Car

◆

## Materials

*1 large box (to fit around child's body)*
*X-acto knife (or other sharp knife)*
*Paints of various colors*
*Black felt-tip pen*
*Stapler*

All you need for this project is a box big enough to fit around a small body.

Cut off bottom and top of box, leaving four sides intact. Cut a small slit on either side to fit hands. Paint box sides a solid color and add detail to make it look like a car, truck, or bus, or whatever you want. Outline separate colors in black to make them stand out. Use box top or bottom to create wheels and staple into place. When car is finished, step inside, hold onto handle slits, and start traveling.

# Box Plane

◆

## Materials

*1 large cardboard box*
*X-acto knife (or other sharp knife)*
*Stapler*
*Enamel spray paint*
*Felt-tip pens (or acrylic paints)*

You can make a 747, a space shuttle, or a biplane with a plain old cardboard box.

Remove the top and bottom of box and cut them into wing shapes (A). Make a slit on either side of box (B) and insert wings (C). Fold over the ends inside box and staple them down securely. Cut a notch on top of slit on either side to fit hand. Spray-paint plane a solid color and add detail with felt-tip pens or acrylic paints. (Try camouflage!) Then blast off. (Using a larger box, try other modes of transportation—boat, rocket, tank, van, cement truck, fire truck, police car, anything!)

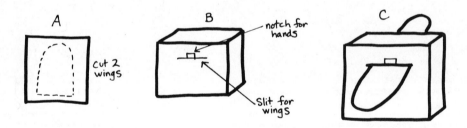

# The Little Engine That Could

◆

## Materials

*4 or more large boxes*
*X-acto knife (or other sharp knife)*
*Cardboard for wheels*
*Stapler (or white glue, such as El-mer's)*
*White enamel spray paint*
*Colored tape, felt-tip pens, paints, de-cals, etc.*
*Skewer*
*Rope, cut into 4-inch pieces*

You'll need 4 or more boxes for this delightful train.

Cut out train shapes, using guide shown (*A*). Cut wheels from scrap card-board and staple or glue to sides of train cars. Spray-paint train white and allow to dry. Add detail with colored tape, felt-tip pens, paints, decals, and so on. To connect cars, poke holes in front and back of each car. Insert short piece of rope and knot so it won't pull through. Repeat until all train cars are connected. Fill with children, toys, dolls, pets, and so on.

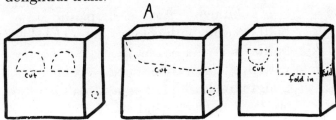

# Street Cleaner

◆

## Materials

*White and red enamel spray paint*
*Cereal box (13-ounce size)*
*Cardboard Band-Aid box*
*White glue (such as Elmer's)*
*4 oatmeal container lids*
*Scissors*
*Cardboard*
*2 chopsticks (or sticks of similar size)*
*4 toothpaste tops*
*Clear plastic spray bottle*
*Food coloring*
*2 large rubber bands*
*Decals, permanent felt-tip pens,*
  *paint, etc.*

This truck is made entirely from household discards, and it really works!

Spray-paint cereal box and cardboard Band-Aid box white (A). Glue Band-Aid box to cereal box as shown (B). Reinforce each round oatmeal container lid by cutting out another circle of the same size from cardboard and gluing it to the inside of the lid to form wheels (C). Spray-paint the wheels red. Make a small hole in the center of each wheel; make 2 small holes in each side of the cereal box where you want the wheels to be. Insert 2 chopsticks or other sticks through the cereal box and stick on the four round oatmeal lid wheels. Cover wooden ends with glue and toothpaste tops (D).

Thoroughly rinse clear plastic spray bottle and fill with colored water (E). Lay bottle on cereal box as shown (F). Secure with two large rubber bands. Add decorations to truck with felt pens, decals, and so on. Paint in truck windows (G).

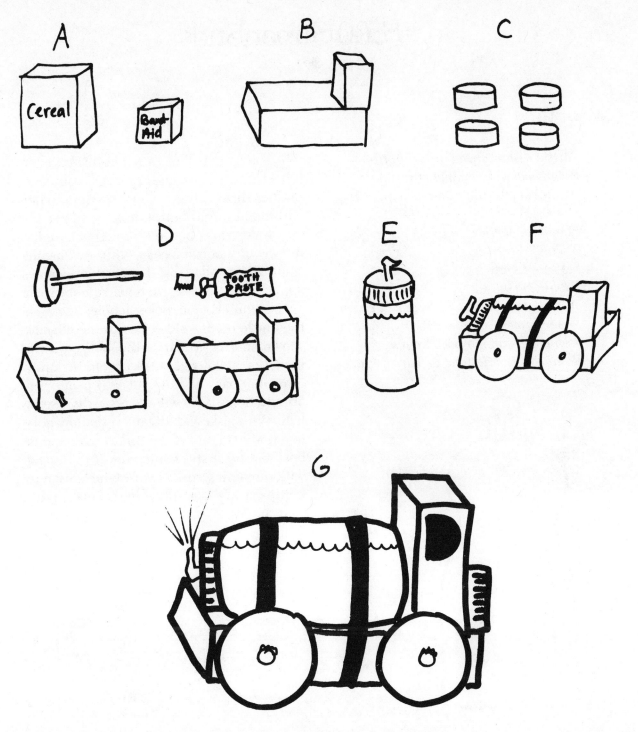

# Indy 500 Super Suds

◆

## Materials

Plastic dishwashing liquid bottle
Bright-colored enamel spray paint
Metal skewer (or other sharp instrument)
Pencil (or metal rod)
2 plastic straws
Serrated knife
2 wine corks
White glue (such as Elmer's) or rubber cement
4 round shampoo bottle caps
Paint (or plastic tape or car striping)

You'll soon have a whole parking lot full of Trans Ams and 280Zs if you save plastic dishwashing soap bottles, wine corks, and round bottle caps.

First, rinse bottle thoroughly and dry it. Give the bottle 2 coats with the enamel spray paint, allowing it to dry after each application. With a sharp instrument such as a metal skewer, poke 4 holes through the bottle on one side close to the edge as shown in (A). Enlarge the holes with a pencil or metal rod. Insert a plastic straw into one pair of holes (B); repeat with other 2 holes. Cut wine corks crosswise in half. With a skewer, dig out a shallow hole in one side of one of the corks. Add glue to hole and twist straw into cork (C). Repeat with remaining cork halves. Glue cork into bottle cap (D) and allow to dry overnight. Repeat. With paint, plastic tape, or car striping, add detail and numbers (E). Vvvrrrooommmmmmmm. . . .

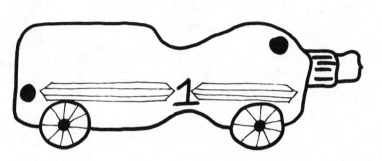

A
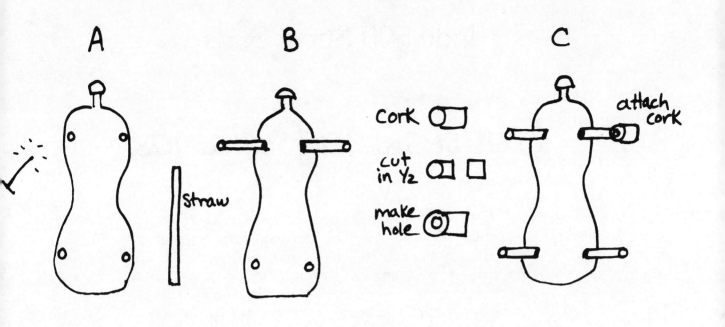

B

cork

cut
in ½

make
hole

C

attach
cork

straw

D

straw      cork      Shampoo
                     cap

E

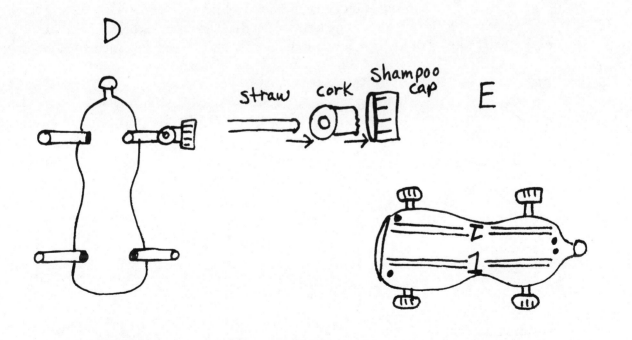

# · 5 ·

# Houses and Buildings

Need a home for all those Strawberry Shortcake miniatures? Or a place for G.I. Joe to bunk? How about something in a larger size—just right to hide in?

This chapter provides several different kinds of structures to allow you to create an environment for dolls and other figures, and larger constructions that will accommodate a little person. Most are made from cardboard, and if you glue two to three pieces of cardboard together, they become nearly indestructible. (I say nearly—*nothing* is indestructible to a child.)

Pick out a few costumes from the Costume Store (Chapter 6) to dress in while playing.

# Country Store

◆

## Materials

*2 large boxes*
*X-acto knife (or other sharp knife)*
*White glue (such as Elmer's)*
*Single-edged razor blade (optional)*
*Masking tape*
*White enamel spray paint*
*Acrylic paints (or felt-tip pens)*
*Scraps of wallpaper and carpet*

The supermarket will supply you with the foundation for your building—for free! Pick two large boxes of equal size. On one box *only*, cut off the top and one side *(A)*. Save the scraps. Cut the 3 standing sides so that a slanting roof foundation is formed as shown *(B)*. Cut scraps into 4 small squares, approximately 1 × 1 inch, and glue them to inside of box about halfway up from bottom *(C)*. Allow to dry. Using your other cardboard box, cut a "second

floor" to fit inside the building, and set floor on support squares *(D)*.

For front detail, cut strips from excess cardboard and glue layers together to create a three-dimensional effect *(E)*. Make beams, posts, awning, and overhang, and glue to front walls *(F)*. Cut out windows with X-acto knife or razor blade *(G)*. Cut off door and tape, on one side, back onto house, so it will open and close *(H)*.

Spray box with 2 coats of white paint, letting each dry before applying the next. Use a picture from a book or magazine, or use your own design, to create exterior decoration with acrylic paints or felt-tip pens *(I)*. Decorate inside with wallpaper scraps and carpet pieces. Attach oversized piece of scrap cardboard to top of building for roof *(J)*.

A

B

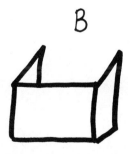

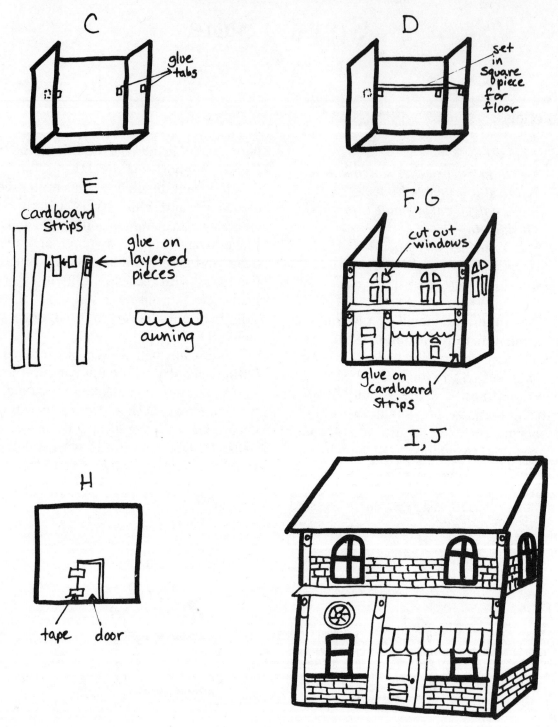

C

glue tabs

D

set in square piece for floor

E

cardboard strips

glue on layered pieces

awning

F, G

cut out windows

glue on cardboard strips

H

tape   door

I, J

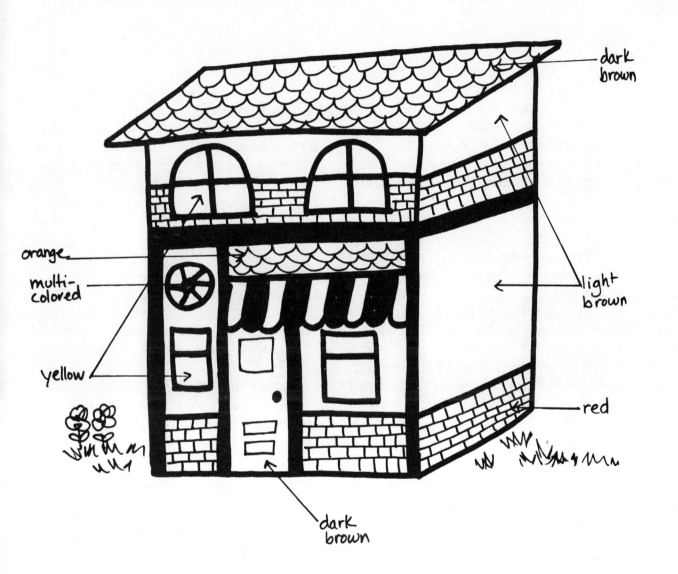

dark
brown

light
brown

orange

multi-
colored

yellow

red

dark
brown

# Chipmunk House

◆

## Materials

*1 large washing-machine-sized box*
*4 large cardboard panels*
*Masking tape (optional)*
*X-acto knife (or other sharp knife)*
*Masking tape (or stapler)*
*Brown and green paint (or wood-grain and green Con-Tact paper)*
*Crayons (or felt-tip pens or poster paint)*

You can make this any type of house or fort you like. This one is especially for chipmunks.

Ask your local appliance store for a large washing-machine-sized box and any 4 large scraps of cut-up boxes, at least 4 inches wider than the width of the big box. (If you have trouble finding scraps that big, tape several large pieces together.) Cut off top of box (and bottom, if you like) and carve out a small curved door, leaving one side still attached. Fold the door open to form a crease (A).

Cut the 4 panels as shown, being sure bottom edge of each is 4 inches wider than width of large box (B). Tape or staple panels together and set on top of large box (C). (This roof is removable and allows light and air in, but can be covered at the top to make it dark inside.)

Paint house brown and outline tree-trunk markings with black crayon or felt-tip pen, or use wood-grain Con-Tact paper. Paint roof green, or cover with green Con-Tact paper, and outline a pattern of overlapping large leaves. Draw kitchen appliances, bedroom furniture, etc., on the inside and color with crayons or felt-tip pens. Add flowers to outside with felt pen or poster paint (D).

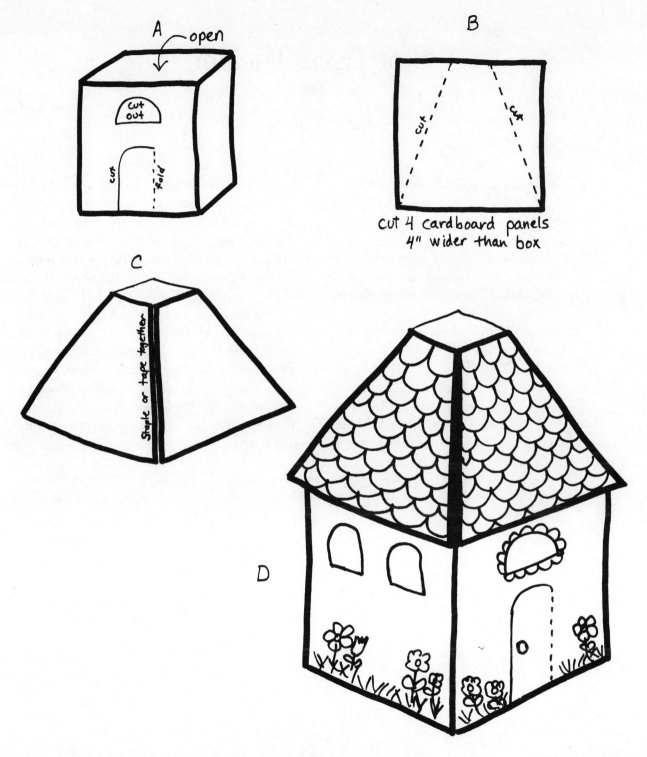

A  open

cut out

cut   fold

B

cut   cut

cut 4 cardboard panels
4" wider than box

C

staple or tape together

D

65

# Storybook Theater

◆

## Materials

*X-acto knife (or other sharp knife)*
*1 large washing-machine-sized box*
*Paint*
*Stapler*
*2 pieces scrap fabric (each approximately 20 × 10 inches)*
*Metal skewer or other sharp instrument (optional)*
*2 pieces (12 inches each) yarn or ribbon (optional)*

Cut back off box and make a large rectangular opening in top half of the box. Paint front and sides to look like a theater or television set. On inside of box, staple two pieces of fabric to cover the opening and serve as curtains. If you want to tie your curtains back, poke 2 small holes in box on either side of the curtains as shown, and pull through a small piece of ribbon or yard; tie back the curtain when it's show time. Or simply flip it up on top of the box.

With a few puppets, put on a play or television program. (This would be a good time to get out the video camera!) You can also use the theater as a post office, a grocery counter, a drive-in restaurant, a drive-through bank, or a photo store. With enough boxes you could have an entire town!

STORYBOOK
THEATRE

inside

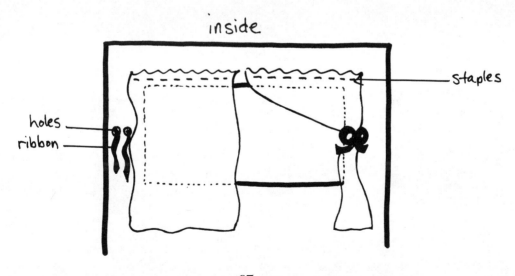

staples

holes
ribbon

# Traveling Condo

◆

## Materials

> *1 large box*
> *X-acto knife (or other sharp knife)*
> *Ruler*
> *Scraps of carpet, Con-Tact paper, and*
>   *wallpaper*
> *Acrylic paints (optional)*

This version of the dollhouse can be packed up and taken to Grandma's.

Find a large box *(A)* at the grocery store and cut it into 3 flat pieces with an X-acto knife *(B)*. Use one large flat piece as the base, or floor, and mark it off into 4 equal sections *(C)*. Cover each section with a different color carpet scrap or Con-Tact paper *(D)*.

Take a second piece of cardboard and make a cut halfway down the center; repeat with another piece of cardboard the same size *(E)*. Invert one piece and slot it into the other, to make 4 walls in an X shape. Mark the walls that intersect at right angles with numbers, as shown *(F)*, and pull apart. Decorate matching numbers with the same wallpaper scraps, paint, or Con-Tact paper; cut out doors. Recut the slots and assemble again. Set walls on top of floor to create open rooms. Add furniture and dolls.

When ready to travel, disassemble the walls. Pack up all parts in a box or suitcase and head for Grandma's house.

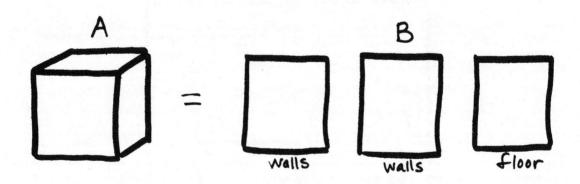

68

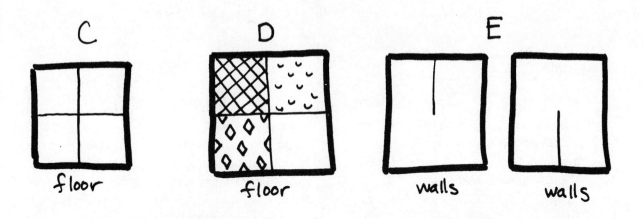

C
floor

D
floor

E
walls          walls

F

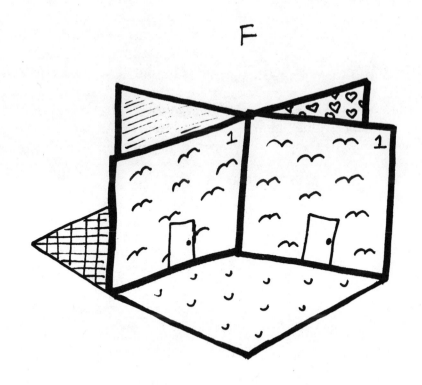

# Swiss Chalet

◆

## Materials

*X-acto knife (or other sharp knife)*
*2 boxes, one larger than the other*
*White glue (such as Elmer's)*
*Masking tape*
*White enamel spray paint*
*Acrylic paints (brown, yellow, red)*
*Black felt-tip pen*
*Brown lace (or braid trim)*
*Single-edge razor blade (optional)*
*Scrap cardboard*
*Flowers cut from fabric trim*

Perfect for Barbie or Strawberry Shortcake.

Cut backs off both boxes (A) and stack larger one on top of smaller; glue them together (B). Allow to dry. Cut top at a slant (C) as foundation for roof, then cut 2 roof pieces a little larger than opening and tape them together (D). Tape roof in place. Spray-paint house white (two coats) and allow to dry. Paint roof brown and outline scallops with felt-tip pen. Glue on brown lace or braid trim along front and side edges.

Cut out windows and doors with X-acto knife or single-edge razor blade. Cut strips of scrap cardboard for shutters and doorframe and paint them brown. Glue them on front of house, as shown. Paint on yellow and red hearts and scrollwork. Glue fabric trim flowers under bottom windows and cover bottom edge of flowers with a strip of brown cardboard.

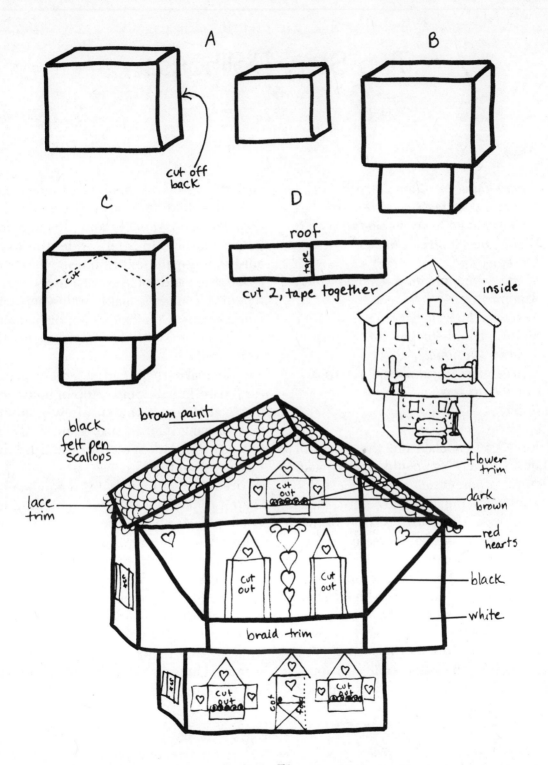

A

cut off
back

B

C

cut

D

roof

tape

cut 2, tape together

inside

brown paint

black
felt pen
scallops

lace
trim

flower
trim

dark
brown

red
hearts

cut
out

cut
out

cut
out

black

white

braid trim

cut
out

cut

cut
out

# Two-Story Dollhouse

◆

## Materials

    *X-acto knife (or other sharp knife)*
    *1 large corrugated cardboard box*
      *(big enough to accommodate a doll)*
    *White glue (such as Elmer's)*
    *Masking tape*
    *White, red, and dark enamel spray*
      *paint*
    *Acrylic paints (or felt-tip pens)*
    *Scraps of wallpaper or Con-Tact*
      *paper (optional)*
    *1 large piece of cardboard for roof*
    *Cardboard scraps*
    *Ruler*

Have you checked out the prices of dollhouses today? You could almost make the down payment on a real house for what they're asking at the toy store. Making your own dollhouse is one of the easiest, cheapest, and most creative things you can do together.

Cut off back of box and cut top at slant as a foundation for roof. With the scraps, cut out a second-story floor. Glue in 1-inch-square scraps of cardboard halfway up the side walls to hold the second floor in place; let dry, then set floor in (see opposite). Cut out two room dividers, one for each floor. Make doors by cutting each on two sides, folding remaining side to allow door to open. Slide room dividers into house and tape to front inside wall to secure. Spray-paint entire house white (two coats), then add color to outside and inside to suit. You can make wallpaper with fabric scraps, Con-Tact paper, or by creating a pattern with felt-tip pens on the white walls.

To make roof, fold a large piece of cardboard in half. Set on top of house and mark off ½ inch extra all the way around for overhang. Cut to size. Paint roof with two coats of dark spray paint and let dry. Place roof on top of house. (If you wish to secure roof, add tape, but you may want to keep it removable.) To make chimney, cut small pieces of cardboard and tape together. Hold chimney box to side of roof at desired height and trace the angle, then cut to fit on roof. Spray paint red; let dry, and tape to top of roof.

Front detail is added by cutting bits of cardboard and gluing them around the windows and doors to make frames. Add as much gingerbread as you like. Fill with doll furniture and dolls.

# The Big City

◆

## Materials

*X-acto knife (or other sharp knife)*
*Several large and small cardboard boxes*
*White glue (such as Elmer's)*
*Small flag (or monkey figure; both available at hobby or toy store)*
*16 small pompons (available at fabric or hobby store)*
*Masking tape*
*Felt-tip pens*
*White enamel spray paint*
*Acrylic paints (optional)*

You can name this collection after your nearby big city and add some familiar local sites to the plan.

1. *The Skyscraper (A).*

Cut back off a large box and cut windows on all sides, as shown. Add floors by gluing 1-inch-square scraps of cardboard to the insides at desired intervals; let dry; then lay a piece of cardboard for each floor on top (see page 62). Find four more boxes, each smaller than the next, to form the tower. Cut off the backs; then cut windows to match those in the large box. Stack and glue boxes to form a pyramid. Place a small flag (or miniature ape, if you want to make the Empire State Building) on top of building. Glue small pompons to corners of box.

2. *High-Rise Apartment Building (B).*

Cut back off a large box and cut out square windows, as shown, and a large double door. Tape doors back on (on the inside) so they can be opened and closed. Add detail with felt-tip pen. Make floors inside the building by cutting out 1-inch-square scraps of cardboard, gluing them inside boxes, and laying pieces of cardboard on top (see page 62).

3. *City Parking (C).*

Cut back off a large box and cut out large rectangular windows. Create 3 or 4 floors on the inside by cutting out 1-inch-square scraps of cardboard, gluing them inside boxes, and laying pieces of cardboard on top (see page 62). Cut a small opening in each floor except for ground floor. Cut out ramps from scrap cardboard and run from opening to lower floor; tape to secure, as shown.

Spray-paint all buildings white (two coats) and allow to dry. Use paint or felt pen to add details to your buildings.

A

B

The Palace

City Parking

C

tape ramp

cut hole

enlarged detail

75

# Camelot Castle

◆

## Materials

*Several small boxes (tea, spice, toilet-*
*ries, etc.)*

*Several cardboard tubes (wrapping*
*paper, foil, paper towel, toilet*
*paper, etc.)*

*Scraps of wrapping paper, Con-Tact*
*paper (or enamel spray paint of*
*various colors)*

*White glue (such as Elmer's)*

*Scraps of gold and braid trim, rick-*
*rack*

*Suit-box lid or large cereal box*

*Masking tape (optional)*

*Scraps of tagboard (or cone-shaped*
*paper cups)*

*Several paper or plastic straws*

*Scraps of ribbon, sequins, glitter, etc.*

When you have collected enough small boxes and tubes, wrap each with different scraps of wrapping paper or Con-Tact paper, or spray-paint them with different colors. Glue gold and braid trim and rickrack around tops of each.

Group tubes together on the top of a suit-box lid or other piece of cardboard and glue or tape into place. Be sure to stack a few, too. Top tubes with inverted cones made from tagboard (see below) or with cone-shaped paper cups. Insert a straw into each cone top and tape or glue on a piece of ribbon cut like a flag. Add sequins, glitter, and so on, for more decoration.

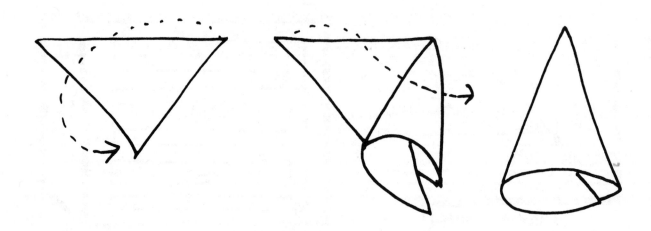

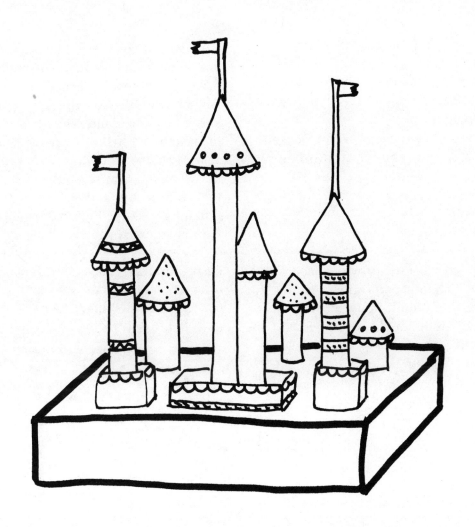

# Secret Fort

◆

## Materials

*Ruler*
*Card table*
*Scissors*
*Old sheet or large piece of leftover fabric*
*Felt-tip pens*
*Crayons or acrylic paints (optional)*
*Sewing machine (or needle and thread)*
*Pinking shears*
*12-inch strip of Velcro*

The secret fort provides a special place in which to play imaginary games, to be alone, to pretend. You can make a secret fort by using an old card table and an old sheet or some leftover fabric.

Measure your table and cut 5 pieces of fabric to cover the top and 4 sides, al-lowing room for seam. Lay each side panel out on floor and using a black felt-tip pen, draw a theme on each panel—one side could be a club house, one a fire station, one a toy store, and one a hospital. Color in designs with felt-tip pens, crayons, or acrylic paints. Add clouds, sun, and moon to top panel. Sew the sides together first, then pin on top and seam together. With pinking shears, cut open door and window flaps at sides, as shown. Sew pieces of Velcro to corners of windows and door and to corresponding places on fort so, when opened, windows and door will stay open.

Spread the sheet over the card table and then use your imagination.

# · 6 ·

# *Fantasy Lands*

Here's an opportunity for you to visit some strange places via imagination. Many of the Fantasy Lands are designed to be used with dolls and figures, while others provide a place for you to visit personally.

When the space movies came out, my husband and I designed the Space Station (page 88) from household trash! We had been saving empty deodorant bottles and discarded orange juice cans for a while, not knowing how we would eventually use them, but not wanting to throw them away. Then my son and daughter saw one of the *Star Wars* epics and decided they wanted to buy every *Star Wars* toy made. Instead, we dumped out the huge box of collected refuse and began to put cans, bottles, and boxes together. Spray-painting everything white gave it a store-bought look, and gave the children an opportunity to decorate as they pleased. The set can be taken apart and stored, then reconstructed, perhaps in a different way, the next time.

If outer space isn't your favorite place, create a familiar town, a Spooky Gold Mine, or open up a Costume Store.

# Your Town, U.S.A.

◆

## Materials

*2 pieces of plywood (each 6 × 3 feet)*
*Green enamel spray paint*
*Gray enamel paint*
*Permanent felt-tip pens*
*White construction paper*
*Scissors*
*White glue (such as Elmer's)*
*Shellac (or verathane)*
*2 hinges (optional)*

*or:*

*2 pieces of green felt (each 6 × 3 feet)*
*Several 12-inch squares of felt in a
    variety of colors*
*Scissors*
*Sewing machine (or needle and
    thread)*
*Permanent felt-tip pens*

My children have been playing in "Danville" since they were toddlers, and the toy still hasn't lost its appeal, some eight years later. My husband designed this open-ended play environment, and it comes out of its storage place at least twice a week. Be sure the whole family helps on this one.

There are two ways to create your town. Paint two 6-by-3-foot pieces of plywood green with enamel spray paint. Design your city on a piece of paper and use it as a model for transferring permanently to the wood. Lay boards side by side and paint on streets with gray paint. Add detail to streets with permanent felt-tip pens for lanes, dividers, and so on. (Use permanent felt-tip pens or colors will bleed when shellacked later.) Include a blue area if you have lakes or rivers nearby. Work together to decide what you want in your town. (My young son was afraid of our real town car wash, so he made three of them for his pretend town—it was a good way to help him conquer his fear!) Draw outlines of stores and houses on white construction paper, cut out, then color with felt-tip pen or crayon for detail. Glue them onto the wood. Give the entire town a coat of shellac or verathane to protect it. Add more items and landmarks as the child grows and other interests develop. (See our design at right.) And you may want to hinge the two pieces of wood together.

If you prefer sewing to woodworking, you can also make your town from fabric. That way it can be folded up and tucked away, rather than slid under the bed, as you might have to do with the wooden town. Sew the two large pieces of felt together to form a 6-by-6-foot square. Cut out, then appliqué the houses, streets, and stores, adding detail with permanent felt-tip pens. My children prefer the wooden town because the cars move more freely on the hard surface and the houses have more detail. But the fabric town is handy for taking on trips.

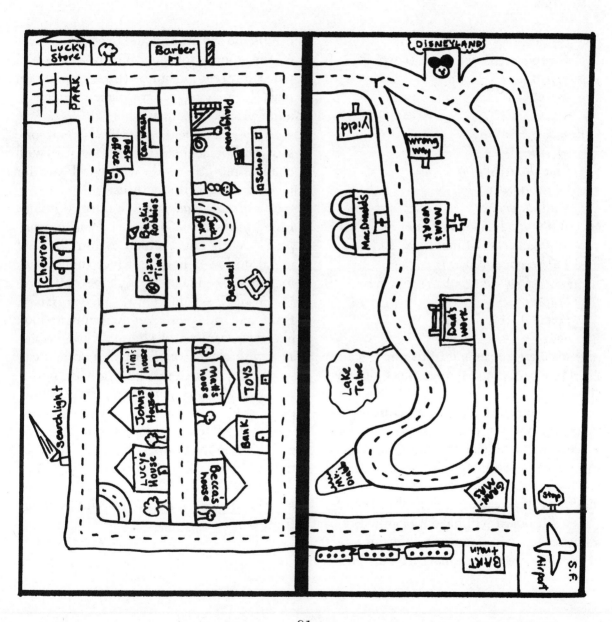

# Cheese House

◆

## Materials

*Jigsaw*
*4 squares of plywood (each 3 × 3 feet)*
*6 hinges*

*Options:*

*Blackboard paint*
*Corkboard*
*Wallpaper*
*White glue (such as Elmer's)*
*Metal sheets (24 inches × 10 inches)*
*Yellow enamel paint*
*Clear Con-Tact paper*
*Stapler*
*Felt*

My children named this one because it reminded them of a huge piece of Swiss cheese.

With a jigsaw, cut out a square in one piece of plywood, a large circle in second piece, several holes in the third, and leave the fourth piece uncut. Buy 6 hinges and hinge 2 pieces of board together with 3 hinges as shown. Repeat for other board.

Each board will have a personality of its own, and will stimulate different kinds of creativity and imagination. The house can be moved around and used in any area of the room, for any purpose—a quiet place for reading and thinking, a secret place for playing, a dark place for resting, a fun place for fantasy.

*Wall 1—The Uncut Wall.* Paint one side with blackboard paint for use with chalk. Line other side with corkboard for tacking up favorite pictures.

*Wall 2—Wall with Square Window.* Line one side with your favorite wallpaper. With glue, attach a thin sheet of metal on lower half to attract things with magnets, like magnetic alphabet letters.

*Wall 3—Wall with Cheese Holes.* Paint one side with yellow paint to look like a large piece of cheese. Cover other side with clear Con-Tact paper so you can write on wall with washable felt-tip pens.

*Wall 4—Wall with Large Hole.* Staple piece of felt over top of hole to cover it. It can be flipped up to reveal hole. You can use this one for puppet shows and the entrance.

Form your Cheese House in the shapes shown opposite for different activities:

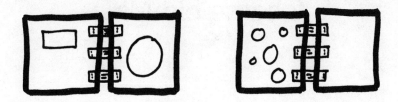

Bird's eye view of set-up options:

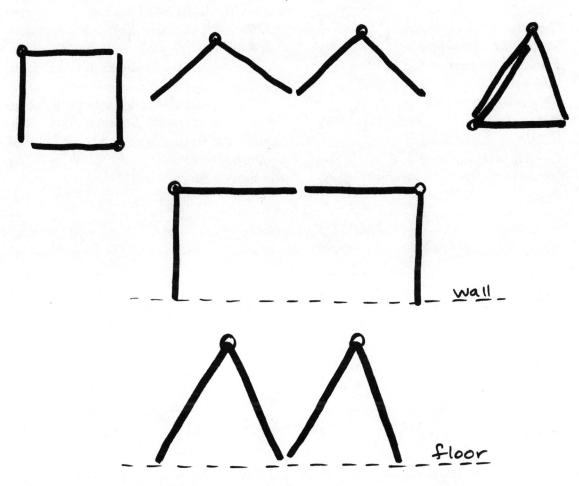

wall

floor

# Spooky Gold Mine

◆

## Materials

*3 or 4 cardboard boxes (large enough*
*  for a child to crawl through)*
*X-acto knife (or scissors)*
*Black enamel spray paint*
*Glitter*
*Glow-in-the-dark paint*
*Several rubber spiders*
*1 yard black yarn*
*Stapler*

Not too spooky—just enough to make it fun.

Line up boxes next to each other and cut openings to create a tunnel. Spray-paint boxes black, inside and out, and while paint is still wet, sprinkle some glitter on the inside. On the inside walls, paint some spooky ghosts or other critters with glow-in-the-dark paint. Buy some rubber spiders at the dime store and tie a piece of black yarn around each one. Staple the other end to the inside ceiling of the cave.

To light up the iridescent paint, shine a light over the paint for several minutes. Then turn out all the lights and travel through the cave. Provide flashlights for the squeamish.

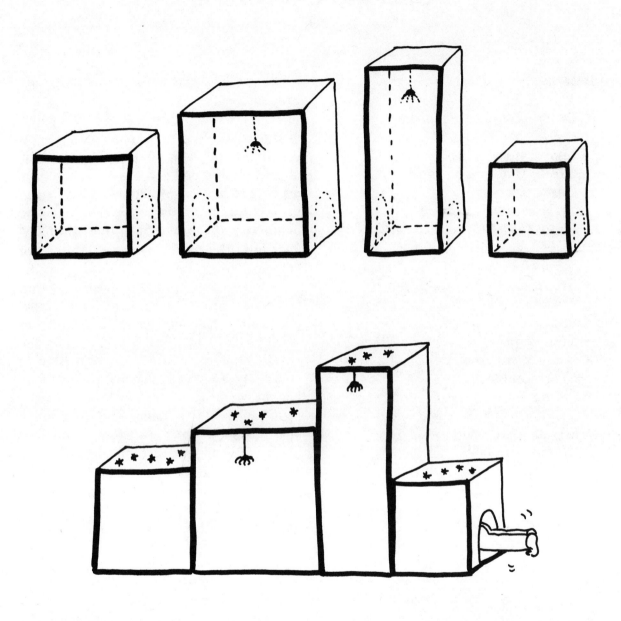

# Dragon Dungeon

◆

## Materials

  *Large sheet of cardboard*
  *Foil*
  *Tape*
  *Green, blue, and black felt-tip pens*
  *Plastic wrap*
  *Large sheet of tagboard*
  *White glue (such as Elmer's)*
  *Stapler and spray-glue adhesive (optional)*
  *Brown, black, and red paint*
  *Scissors*
  *Red tissue paper*
  *1 box (2 inches square)*
  *Gold enamel spray paint*
  *1 yard gold braid*
  *Cotton balls*
  *Sequins (or small beads)*
  *Several small cardboard boxes*
  *Glitter*
  *1 yard black felt*
  *Large sheet of foil*
  *Dragons, monsters, and heroes*

Here's a fantasy land setup for use with medieval and mythical characters and monsters.

*Base.* Cover large flat piece of cardboard with foil and color with green and blue felt-tip pens. Cover the foil with plastic wrap, and color with the same felt-tip pens.

1. *Volcano.* Curve a lightweight piece of tagboard into a cone shape and glue or staple closed. Paint cone brown or black on the outside and red on the inside. Set on base to use as volcano. Cut long triangular pieces of red tissue paper and glue to inside of volcano mouth so that tips hang over the side of the mountain to form hot lava.

2. *Treasure.* Spray-paint 2-inch-square box gold and trim with gold braid. Line with cotton balls and fill with sequins or small beads.

3. *Dungeon.* Cut top off a small cardboard box. Cut bars as shown to form jail-like dungeon. Paint box black.

4. *Caves.* Cut some small cardboard boxes as shown to form caves. Paint box black inside and out. Dot inside with glue or use spray-glue adhesive and sprinkle with glitter. Cut out long triangles from black felt and glue inside cave roof to hang down like stalactites. Color a large sheet of foil with black felt-tip pen and gently wrinkle it. Use glue to attach foil to top of cardboard box to form sharp craggy peaks on cave.

Add dragons, monsters, and heroes.

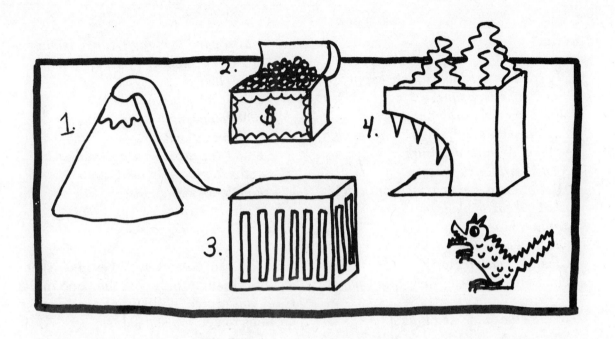

# Space Station

◆

## Materials

Plywood or cardboard base (approximately 4 feet square)

White enamel spray paint

Acrylic paints (or felt-tip pens, plastic tape, or auto striping)

Small cardboard box

X-acto knife (or scissors or single-edged razor blade)

Potato-chip can

Clear plastic bowl

Clear or masking tape

Long cardboard wrapping-paper tube

White glue (such as Elmer's)

Styrofoam egg carton (or plastic popsicle holders, ice cube trays, or halves of L'Eggs-type pantyhose containers)

4 L'Eggs-type pantyhose containers (silver, gold, black, or clear are best)

Cardboard or plastic shoebox

4 large frozen orange juice cans

4 Tickle-type deodorant bottles

Aluminum pie pan

Round oatmeal container

Empty 12-ounce can

Odd-shaped Styrofoam packing pieces (or small cardboard box)

Cardboard rectangle (approximately 24 × 3 inches)

Pipe cleaner

T bracket (optional)

Small spaceman dolls

1 rubber glove

Small (approximately 4 inches in diameter) needlepoint hoop

Plastic drinking glass

4 "crazy straws"

Small empty can

You can create an "awesome" space station, limited only by the amount of trash you can collect! Here are some suggestions to get you started:

Begin with a plywood or cardboard base, painted with white enamel spray paint and detailed with futuristic stripes using acrylic paint, felt-tip pen, plastic tape, or auto striping (A, page 90).

*1. Landing Base.* Set a small cardboard box upside down for foundation of landing base (B). Cut out curves from base (C) and paint box white. Set potato-chip can, painted white, on top of box and borrow a clear plastic bowl from the cupboard to set on top of can (D). Tape a cardboard wrapping-paper tube to top of bowl (E). Add Styrofoam egg carton, plastic Popsicle holders, ice cube trays, or halves of

L'Eggs-type pantyhose containers to top of box (F).

2. *Decontamination Center.* Cut openings in a shoebox or buy a clear plastic shoebox (G) and place 4 frozen orange juice cans inside the corners (H). (You can also use taller cans, such as for potato chips, and place them inside corners of box.) Spray box and cans white and add detail with felt-tip pen (I). Take apart two Tickle-type deodorant bottles and glue cylinders together (J). Top with a L'Eggs-type pantyhose container (K). Set in center of box. Flank this tower with the other two of the deodorant bottles (L).

3. *Control Tower.* Place aluminum pie pan upside down on base (M). Cut openings as shown in round oatmeal container and place on pan (N). Glue 12-ounce can to top of oatmeal container and glue L'Eggs-type pantyhose container to top of can (O). Spray white and add detail with felt-tip pen (P).

4. *Computer Center.* Use some large Styrofoam pieces from last year's Christmas garbage (or a small cardboard box sprayed white and cut out), to form base (Q). Cut cardboard ramp and place between Control Tower and Computer Center (R). Glue L'Eggs-type pantyhose container to top of Styrofoam or cardboard (S).

To make "pod" poke a small hole in one end of a L'Eggs-type container and hook in a pipe cleaner (T). Attach other end of pipe cleaner around plastic circle removed from Tickle-type bottle and slip circle onto tube (U). Attach loose end of cardboard tube to top of Computer Center with tape or T bracket. Slide pod, with passengers (small dolls) inside, up and down cardboard tube.

5. *Launch Pad.* Cut a rubber glove into a large, open piece and stretch in a needlework hoop (V). Trim rubber and set on plastic drinking glass (W). Bounce spacemen dolls on pad (X).

6. *Power Cables.* Place "crazy straws" in small can that has been painted white. Add detail to can (Y).

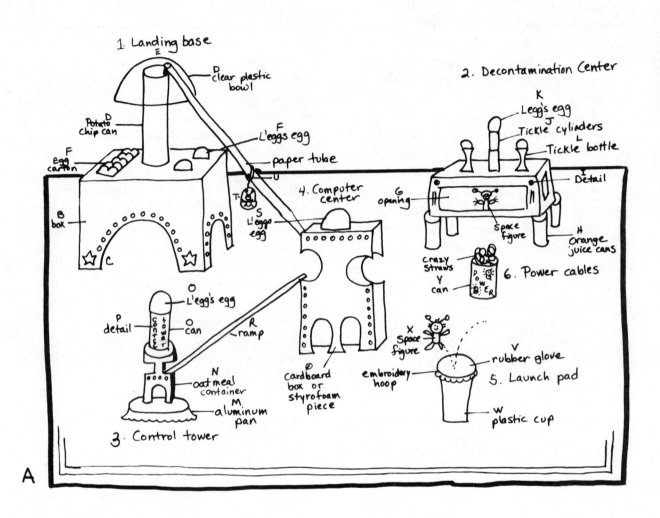

1. Landing base

E

D clear plastic bowl

D Potato chip can

F L'eggs egg

paper tube
U

F egg carton

B box

T

S L'eggs egg

C

4. Computer center

2. Decontamination Center

K Legg's egg

J Tickle cylinders

L Tickle bottle

I Detail

G opening

Space figure

H orange juice cans

crazy straws

Y can

P O W E R

6. Power cables

O L'egg's egg

P detail

O can

R ramp

N oatmeal container

M aluminum pan

3. Control tower

Ø cardboard box or styrofoam piece

X Space figure

embroidery hoop

V rubber glove

5. Launch pad

W plastic cup

A

# Costume Store

◆

## Materials

*Clothing and accessories from thrift
 shops*
*Large box*

The Costume Store is probably my
children's favorite fantasy. In it they can
be whomever they wish.

Visit your local Goodwill, Salvation
Army, St. Vincent de Paul, or other thrift
store. You can make a few dollars go a long
way and help support a good cause at the
same time. Pick out a wide variety of
clothing and accessories.

*1. The Shoe Department.* How about
some gold lamé high heels, a pair of war-
torn soldier boots, some black patent-
leather tap-dance shoes, some ballet slip-
pers, or some ladies' boots?

*2. The Millinery Department.* It's
amazing how a child becomes transformed
by a new hat! Try a netted number, a Boy
Scout hat, a "Carmen Miranda" hat with
lots of fruit and flowers, and a beanie.
Also, don't forget to pick up a couple of
wigs—short and curly or long and straight,
blond, brunette, black, or red.

*3. The Accessory Department.* Here
you'll find cheap costume jewelry: pearl
necklaces, dangling clip-on earrings,
rhinestone brooches, silk scarves, white
gloves, fur collars, and cowboy belts.

*4. Ladies' Wear.* Pick out some silky
nightgowns that can serve as princess
dresses, short skirts that make long skirts,
and maybe a silly girdle to laugh about.

*5. Men's Wear.* A vest, some baggy
pants, a motorcycle jacket, and an army
shirt all help to make creative outfits.

Stuff everything in a big box and pull
it out on rainy days. Be sure to have the
camera ready.

# People Panels

◆

## Materials

*X-acto knife (or other sharp knife)*
*1 large washing-machine-sized box*
*Permanent felt-tip pens*
*Acrylic paints (optional)*

Fun to make, fun to wear, and great for a photo session.

Cut a washing machine or refrigerator carton into single sheets of cardboard. Near the top of each, cut out a face hole, and below that, 2 holes for arms. Outline different characters in black felt-tip pen and paint or color in clothes, costumes, fur, etc.

When ready, slip arms through armholes and face into face hole, and become a new character!

## Suggestions for people panels

| | |
|---|---|
| *Astronaut* | *Mermaid* |
| *Monster* | *Clown* |
| *Cowboy* | *Mother* |
| *Ballet dancer* | *Baby* |
| *Police officer* | *Father* |
| *Superhero* | *Animal* |
| *Cartoon character* | *Witch* |

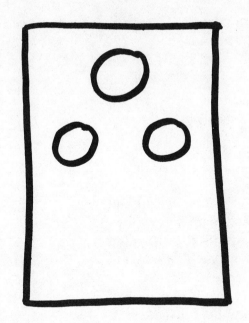

# • 7 •

# *Indoor Toys*

Save this chapter for when the weather is bad and school is out. It's the perfect time to create a new plaything. The making of the project results in a learning experience as well as a fun toy, and can provide hours of creative fun.

With Indoor Toys you can entertain with a couple of clowns, build a high-rise from a number of materials, play a tune, or watch the stars.

# Sewing Cards

◆

## Materials

*Styrofoam grocery tray*
*Scissors*
*Picture from magazine or children's*
　*book*
*White glue (such as Elmer's)*
*Metal skewer (or sharp pencil)*
*Scrap of colorful yarn*
*Large dull needle*

Here's a toy that's short on preparation and long on fun. Clean and dry a Styrofoam grocery tray thoroughly. Cut out an interesting magazine picture and glue it to the tray. With a skewer or sharp pencil, poke a hole every inch along the outlines of the picture. Thread some colorful yarn into a large dull needle and sew through the holes. Repeat as often as you like, using a different picture for each card.

# Clatter Blocks

◆

## Materials

*Leftover wood scraps (or tagboard or*
*cereal boxes or shoeboxes)*
*Saw (or scissors)*
*White glue, such as Elmer's (optional)*
*Acrylic paint (or felt-tip pen)*
*3 shoe laces (each 22 inches long),*
*preferably decorative*
*Staple gun*

Here's an old-fashioned toy that's
scarce today! Make friends with your local
lumberyard or find some leftover wood
scraps from the woodpile and, with your
parents' help, *carefully* saw them into six
3-by-2-inch rectangles—or cut enough
rectangles (about 18) of the same size from
tagboard or cereal boxes or shoeboxes until you have enough to make 6 chips about
¼ inch thick when stacked; glue together
(*A*). Color chips with paint or felt-tip pen
(*B*). Line them up and weave one of the
shoelaces between the pieces as shown
(*C*). Repeat, using two other laces, in an
opposite weave (*D*). Separate the chips so
that they are ¼ inch apart. Carefully
staple the laces to the end chips (*E*). Flip
blocks back and forth and watch each one
tumble down.

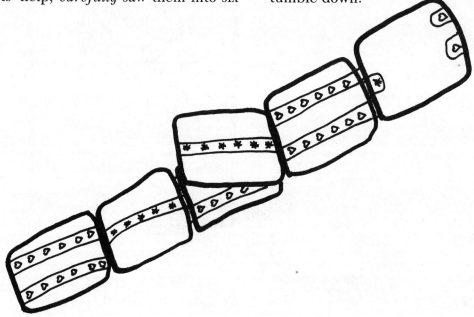

A

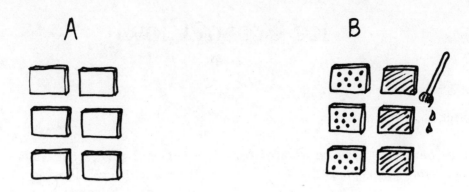

B

C

D

E

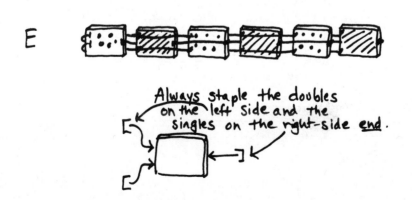

Always staple the doubles on the left side and the singles on the right-side end.

# Ice Cream Clown

◆

## Materials

*Small piece of heavy cardboard (or an empty yarn spool)*
*Scissors*
*½ yard brightly colored fabric*
*White glue (such as Elmer's)*
*1 wooden dowel (¼ inch in diameter, 18 inches long)*
*1 wooden ball (1 inch in diameter) with a hole in it (or a Styrofoam ball)*
*Scraps of yarn*
*Permanent felt-tip pen*
*Needle and thread (optional)*

Bring the Ice Cream Clown to life from his hiding place, or play "peek-a-boo" with baby.

Make a cone from heavy cardboard (see opposite), leaving a hole in the small end, or ask the yarn store for an empty yarn spool (they are cone-shaped and made from thick cardboard) (A).

Cut 2 pieces of "clownish" fabric to fit around cone, allowing ¼ inch to fold over ends. Glue one piece of fabric to cone (B). Apply glue to dowel and insert it in the wooden or Styrofoam ball to form a head and body (C). Glue on yarn hair at the top and make a clown face with permanent felt-tip pen as shown (D).

Sew or glue second piece of fabric into a cone shape. Glue the base of this fabric piece just ½ inch inside of cardboard base, right side out (E). Insert wooden dowel through the top hole of the fabric cone, pulling it through until end of dowel emerges from hole at small end of cardboard base and ball reaches the fabric. Glue fabric to bottom of ball (F). Let clown dry thoroughly.

When ready, pull the dowel down and the clown head will hide in the cone. Push it up gently and twist it around to make it come to life (G).

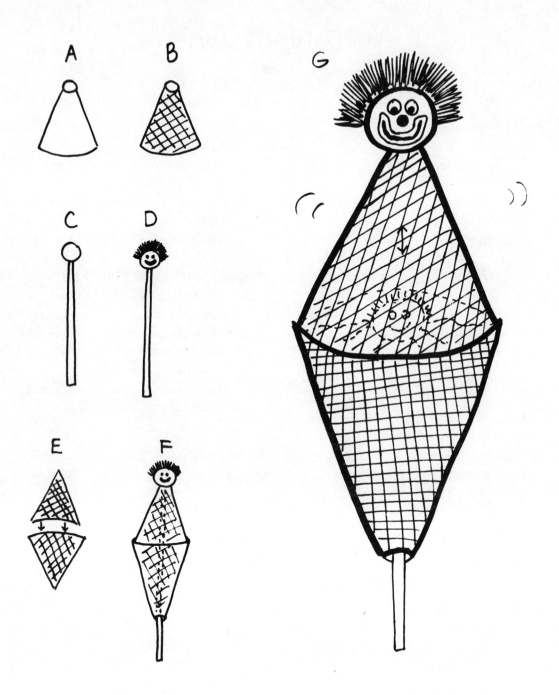

A    B

C    D

E    F

G

99

# Tipsy Clown

◆

## Materials

*L'Eggs-type pantyhouse container or plastic egg (available at hobby store)*
*½ cup sand*
*Masking tape*
*Scissors*
*Scrap of felt (12 inches square)*
*Small sheet of tagboard (or side of cereal box)*
*White glue (such as Elmer's)*
*Felt-tip pen*

Open egg *(A)* and fill bottom half with sand *(B)*. Close the egg and secure all the way around opening with tape *(C)*. Cut out clown from felt, using pattern *(D)*. Cut out a piece of tagboard in same pattern. Glue felt to tagboard, fold in half, and glue tagboard closed. Cut out felt and a piece of tagboard from the half-circle pattern on page 102 *(E)*. Glue felt to tagboard. Make cuts as shown and form into cone, applying glue as shown *(E, F)*. Insert clown into skirt and glue together *(G)*. Glue skirt to top of egg and allow to dry *(H)*. Add detail to face with felt-tip pen.

Lightly push clown and watch him wiggle around.

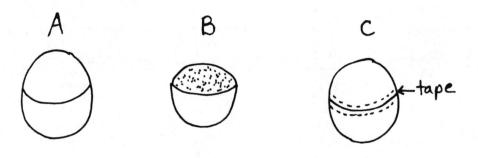

A          B          C

←tape

E

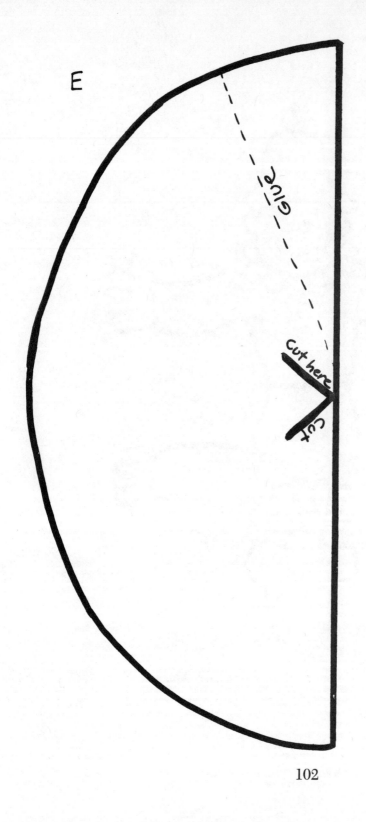

F

G

H

102

# Galaxy Gazing

◆

## Materials

*Scissors*
*Round oatmeal carton*
*Small sheet of tagboard (or side of*
 *cereal box)*
*Constellation chart*
*Straight pin*
*Clear tape*
*Flashlight*

At the end of an active day, here's a perfect bedtime activity.

Cut bottom out of oatmeal carton, leaving a ¼-inch rim *(A)*. Make several circles from tagboard a little larger than the cut-off bottom so they can fit inside the oatmeal box without falling through. Find a constellation chart in an encyclopedia or astronomy book and make some simple constellations by poking a pin through the tagboard circles. Each pinhole makes a "star." Make several different constellations *(B)*.

At night, while lying in bed, turn the bedroom into a planetarium by turning off all the lights, dropping in one of the constellation circles, and taping it in lightly. Put a flashlight into the oatmeal box and aim it at the ceiling *(C)*. You should be able to see your newly created galaxy.

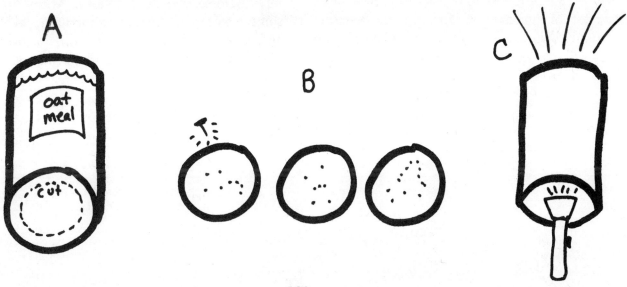

# Build-It Construction Kits

◆

## Materials

*Multicolored toothpicks*
*Frozen peas*

*or:*

*Styrofoam chips*
*Wooden skewers*
*Scissors*

*or:*

*Popsicle sticks*
*Baker's clay (2 cups flour, ½ cup salt,*
  *1 cup less 2 tablespoons water),*
  *Playdo, or modeling clay*

A little fine motor coordination and a lot of imagination go into construction toys. There are two types of materials you will need—the building part and the stick-'em part.

*1. Picks 'n' Peas.* With a collection of multicolored toothpicks and frozen peas, you can create a fantastic high-rise or a simple box. After your construction is complete, allow peas to dry overnight and they will harden. (Feel free to eat some peas along the way.)

*2. Styro-Skewers.* Save Styrofoam chips from Christmas packaging or purchase some from the hobby store. Buy a package of thin wooden skewers from the grocery store and cut them in half with scissors. Cut off the sharp ends for younger children. Skewer the Styrofoam to create your monstrosity/objet d'art.

*3. Popsicle Sticks and Playclay.* By now I'm sure you've saved a pile of Popsicle sticks, but if you aren't a pack rat, you can buy them at the hobby store. Make up some baker's clay by mixing the flour, salt, and water and kneading it well, or use store-bought Playdo or clay to mortar your sticks together. If you use baker's clay, it will dry hard overnight.

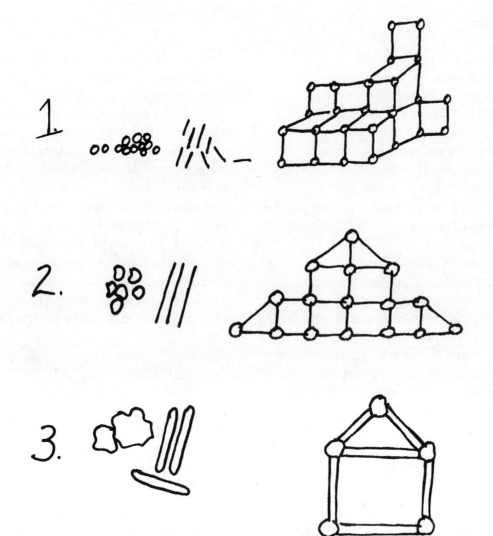

1.

2.

3.

# Kaleidoscope

◆

## Materials

*Scissors*
*Small piece of cardboard*
*Piece of Mylar (8 × 6 inches)*
*White glue (such as Elmer's)*
*Clear tape*
*Hammer and nail*
*Potato-chip (or tennis-ball) can*
*Tissue*
*Confetti (make your own by cutting
   up different colors of construction
   paper)*
*Sandwich baggie*
*Sheet of white paper*

Mylar is used in place of mirrors in this kaleidoscope. You can buy Mylar by the sheet or yard at plastics stores, hardware stores, and sporting goods shops.

Cut piece of cardboard into 3 pieces, each 8 inches long by 2 inches wide *(A)*. Cut 3 pieces of Mylar the same size and glue each onto one side of each cardboard piece. Tape the 3 pieces together to form a triangle with the Mylar on the inside *(B)*.

Punch a nail hole large enough to see through into the bottom of the potato-chip or tennis-ball can *(C)*. Remove plastic lid and insert Mylar triangle. Fill in outer spaces with tissue *(D)*.

Cut up confetti and place in baggie *(E)*. Seal bag with clear tape and place it over open end of tube, making sure confetti is over tube, as shown *(F)*. Cover end with plain white paper and tape tightly to can.

Slowly turn the can as you look through the hole.

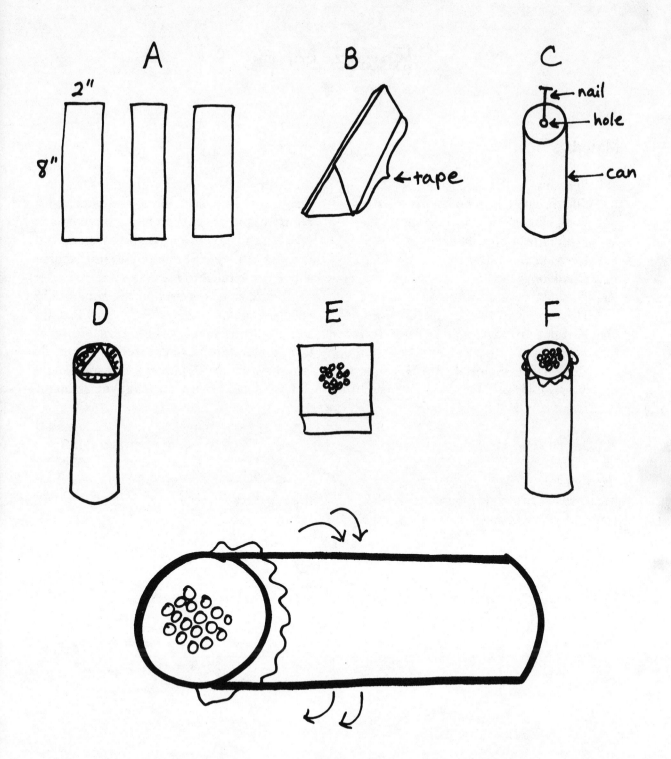

A

2"

8"

B

tape

C

nail

hole

can

D

E

F

107

# Sticker Magic

◆

## Materials

*Scissors*
*Old popped beachball, air mattress,*
*    or plastic inner tube*
*Heavy-duty plastic wrap*
*Large cookie sheet*
*Clear tape*

Here's a way to recycle those inflatable summer toys that barely seem to last the season.

Cut plastic material into the following: various shapes for very young children, the alphabet or numbers for the preschooler, and cartoon characters with plenty of props for storytelling.

Wrap heavy-duty plastic wrap around the smooth back surface of a large cookie sheet. Tape ends to front side.

Place your cutouts on the back of the covered cookie sheet and spell words, do some arithmetic, or just play with the fantasy figures you have created. The plastic cutouts stick to the plastic wrap and can be removed and used over and over again.

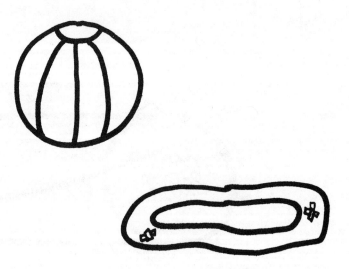

# Jigsaw Puzzle

◆

## Materials

*Picture (from old book), poster, photo, or artwork*
*Spray adhesive (or white glue, such as Elmer's)*
*Sheet of heavy tagboard (or cardboard), same size as picture*
*Clear Con-Tact paper*
*Broad-tipped permanent felt-tip pen*
*Scissors*
*Large manila envelope*

Puzzles are very expensive to buy these days and yet they are so easy to create at home.

Select picture from a favorite old book, buy small poster, enlarge a family photo, or make your own artwork. Spray adhesive or paint a thin coat of glue onto heavy tagboard or cardboard and lay picture on glue. Allow to dry thoroughly. Cover with a sheet of clear Con-Tact paper for added protection. With felt-tip pen, outline puzzle pieces; cut along lines. Make the puzzle as easy or as difficult as you like. Store each puzzle in a large, labeled manila envelope.

# Teeny People

◆

## Materials

*Acrylic paints (or felt-tip pens)*
*Package of round-headed wooden*
*clothespins*
*Fine-tipped felt-tip pens for detail*
*White glue (such as Elmer's)*
*Several different colored pompons*
*(available at fabric or hobby store)*
*Scraps of felt*
*Scissors*
*Cardboard box*

Miniatures are fun to play with, and these Teeny People are just the right size for small hands.

Color the clothespins with acrylic paints or felt-tip pens to suit each character you create. Use fine-tipped felt-tip pens for facial features. Glue pompons to top of heads and glue on felt as arms. Allow to dry.

When ready to play, cut a cardboard box down on the sides so the Teeny People can straddle it.

# Alphabet Blocks

◆

## Materials

*20 or more milk cartons of varying
  sizes
X-acto knife (or scissors)
Masking tape
White, red, blue, and yellow enamel
  spray paint
Alphabet letters, numbers, or pic-
  tures, and white glue, such as El-
  mer's (or permanent felt-tip pen)
Verathane (optional)*

Blocks seem so simple, yet they develop skills necessary for reading and writ-
ing, for cognitive growth, and for fine- and
gross-motor practice. And you can make
your own collection of brightly colored,
educational blocks.

Save milk cartons in the quart, half-
gallon, and pint size until you have at least
twenty *(A)*. Cut off the top of a milk carton. With an X-acto knife or scissors, make
a slit down each corner of the carton *(B)*.
Fold down the flaps to close off the box.
Tape with masking tape *(C)*. Repeat with
all the milk cartons, making some square
and some rectangular for variety.

When your collection of blocks is
finished, spray-paint them all with a white
undercoat, then spray them the primary
colors—red, yellow, and blue. When dry,
glue on letters, numbers, or pictures on all
sides, or write the letters in permanent
felt-tip pen. (You can buy alphabet books
with cute pictures to go with them if
you have no artistic ability. Just cut and
glue them on.) Apply verathane for added
protection.

A

B

C

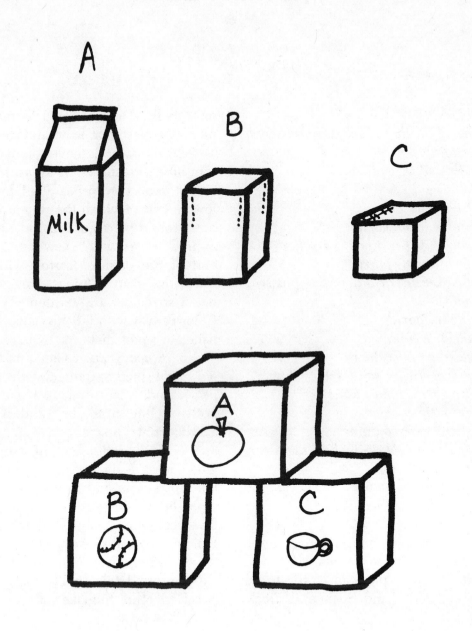

# Marching Band

◆

## Materials

*Scissors*
*Piece of elastic (9 inches long, 1 inch wide)*
*Needle and thread*
*3 bells*
*Felt-tip pens*
*Round oatmeal carton*
*X-acto knife (or other sharp knife)*
*¼ yard canvas fabric*
*Metal skewer (or other sharp instrument)*
*String (or yarn)*
*Small stick (optional)*
*Metal spice containers*
*Rice, dried peas, sand, etc.*
*White glue (such as Elmer's)*
*Acrylic paints*
*Plastic yogurt container*
*1 wooden dowel (½ inch in diameter, 10 inches long)*
*2 sheets of sandpaper*
*2 small blocks of wood*

Create your own one-man band with the following musical instruments:

*1. Bells.* Cut a piece of elastic to fit around your child's hand. Seam ends. Tack on 3 bells. Decorate elastic with felt-tip pen. Slip elastic on hand and shake.

*2. Tomtom.* Remove top and cut bottom off oatmeal carton. Measure opening of carton on piece of canvas fabric and allow an extra inch all the way around. Cut out 2 round pieces of canvas. Punch holes around edges with skewer. Cover each end of the oatmeal carton with canvas. Lace the canvas pieces together with heavy string or yarn; tighten as you finish. Color canvas with felt-tip pens. Beat with hands or small stick.

*3. Spice Shaker.* Clean and then fill old metal spice containers with rice, dried peas, sand, and so on, to make different noises. Glue tops shut and paint with acrylic paints. Shake.

*4. Shaker Rattle.* Finish up the yogurt and save the container. Poke a small hole in bottom and insert a small dowel. Open lid and fill with rice, peas, etc. Glue lid to container. Paint with acrylic paints. Hold dowel and shake.

*5. Sandpaper Sounders.* Glue sandpaper around two small blocks of wood. Brush together to make sound.

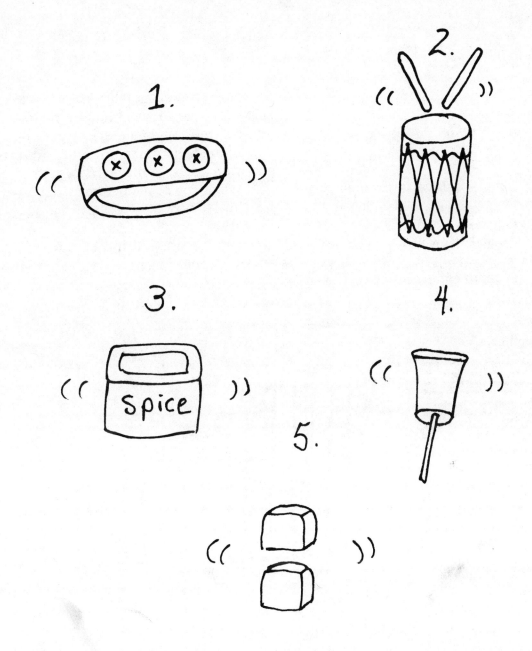

1.

2.

3.

4.

5.

# Peter Pan's Pipes

◆

## Materials

*Ruler*
*Scissors*
*8 plastic drinking straws*
*Masking tape*

This simple musical instrument can be made in seconds and can be played several different ways.

Cut the first straw at 1 inch, the second at 2 inches, and so on, until all 8 have been cut in an ascending order, as shown (A). Lay straws on table in order from smallest to longest and line up the uncut edges *evenly*. Wrap all eight with a piece of masking tape. Move down to next level and wrap again, as shown (B).

When you're ready to play the pipes, hold them next to your lips, flat against your chin. For musical variety, lift the pipes up toward your lips or close up the ends with your fingers.

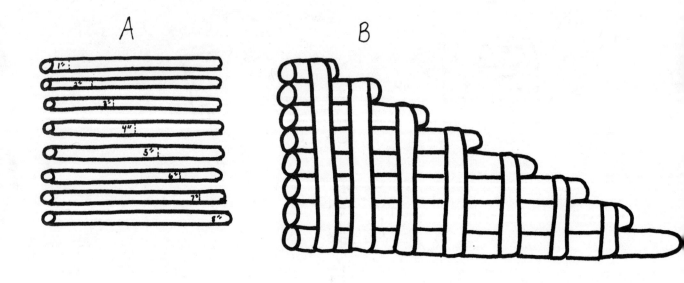

# Long-Distance Hose Phone

◆

## Materials

*Scissors*
*Old garden hose*
*Plastic tape*
*2 plastic bottles (catsup, shampoo,*
  *etc.) (or 2 funnels)*

The toy telephone is always a favorite.

Cut old garden hose into any length you like. Repair any holes in the hose with plastic tape wrapped around several times. Remove tops of 2 plastic bottles and insert hose ends; tape securely with plastic tape. Repeat with other bottle. Cut out 2 holes on side of each bottle—one for listening and one for talking.

You can make a simpler telephone by putting 2 funnels in either end of the hose and taping them in securely.

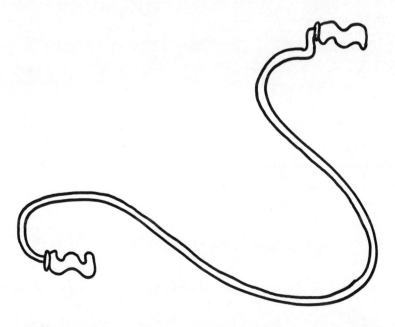

# • 8 •

# *Outdoor Toys*

Why is it that, with the best plaything in the world waiting just outside the door, my kids would rather lie around the house and tell me how bored, bored, bored, bored, bored they are?

The plaything? The out-of-doors, of course. Daily outdoor time is important. You need to absorb some of that natural vitamin, the sun, smell the flowers, and get that all-important large motor exercise you can't get in the house. It's time to go outside, kids. And Mom, take a good look at them. With a handful of Outdoor Toys under their arms, you probably won't see them again until dinner.

# Cup Catcher

◆

## Materials

*Metal skewer (or other sharp instrument)*
*Plastic yogurt container*
*Scissors*
*2-foot piece of yarn, heavy thread, or string*
*Masking tape*
*Eraser, heavy button, walnut, or other small item*

Here's one for the day when there is no one to play with.

Poke a hole in bottom of yogurt container with skewer. Cut a 2-foot-long piece of yarn or string and thread it through hole; tie a knot at end to keep it from pulling through hole. Tape knot down to bottom of cup and secure it. Tie other end to an eraser or some other small item. Now try to flip object into cup.

Make this same toy using smaller containers for older children and larger containers for younger children.

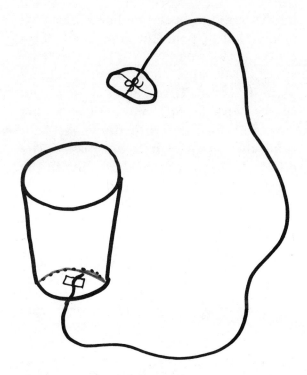

# Jai Alai

◆

## Materials

*2 large bleach bottles*
*Permanent felt-tip pen*
*Scissors*
*Old tennis ball*

The pitching cups, or *cestas,* are made from bleach bottles, so it won't cost you a cent to make this exciting game of skill.

*Thoroughly* clean two large bleach bottles and draw a cutting line with a permanent felt-tip pen. Cut along line to form a scoop-shaped cup.

To play: Find an old tennis ball and place it in one cup. Stand a few feet apart—closer for little ones, farther for big kids. First player has to throw the ball, using the cesta, to the other player. The other player must catch the ball with the cesta. *No hands!*

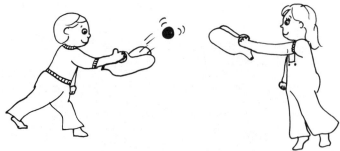

# Miniature Basketball

◆

## Materials

*Wood block (approximately 4 × 4 × 2 inches) for base*
*Hammer and nails*
*Wooden stick (approximately 2 inches in diameter and as tall as you'd like your basket to be)*
*Another block of wood, larger than the first*
*Scissors*
*Sheet of cardboard (approximately 3 × 3 feet square)*
*Staple gun*
*Round ice cream carton, fried chicken container, or paint bucket (cardboard or plastic)*
*Netting (1 yard) or yarn strands (24 12-inch strands)*
*White paint*
*Nerf-type ball*

Find the wooden block to use as base and nail the stick in the center with a long nail from underside. Nail base to another large, sturdy block of wood.

Cut out the baseboard in semicircular shape from a cardboard sheet. Nail or staple baseboard to top end of stick. Cut 2 inches off rim of ice cream carton to form circle. Staple netting or yarn to circle. Staple "basket" to bottom edge of baseboard. Paint cardboard white.

Use a Nerf-type ball with this mini-basketball construction.

# Racquet Ball

◆

## Materials

*Old coat hanger*
*Old nylon stocking*
*Nerf-type balls or sponges (or old socks and foam rubber, cotton balls, torn pantyhose, plastic bread bags, and needle and thread)*
*Rope*

It's easy to make your own racquets and balls for a rousing game of driveway racquet ball.

Bend an old coat hanger into an oval, racquet shape *(A)*. Twist ends together to make a handle *(B)*. Pull old nylon stocking over top and wrap rest of it tightly around handle to make it secure and easy to hold *(C)*.

Hit Nerf-type balls or sponges, or make your own: Stuff old socks with foam rubber, cotton balls, torn pantyhose, or plastic bread bags, and sew them shut *(D)*. Put up a makeshift net by stringing a heavy rope from a couple of trees. Or bat the balls against the garage door.

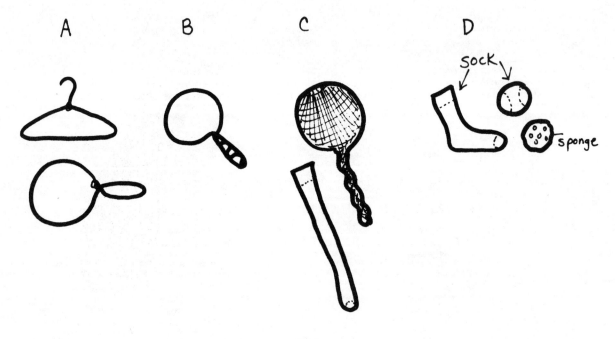

A    B    C    D

sock

sponge

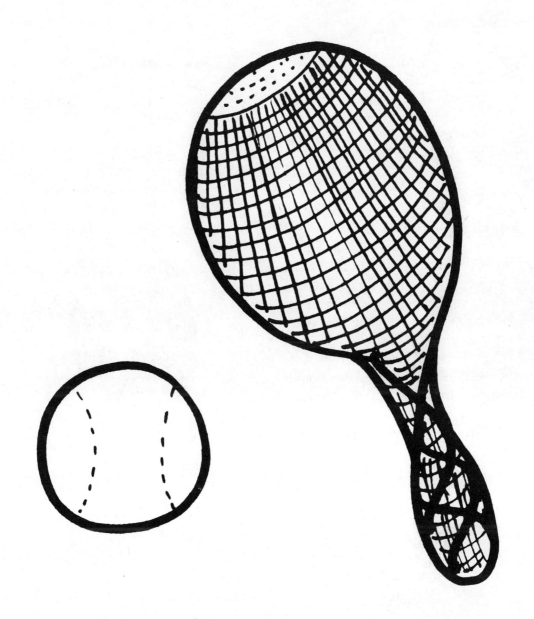

# Comfy Tire Swing

◆

## Materials

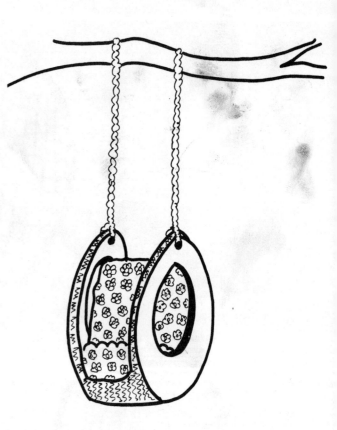

*Old worn tire (wide enough to fit child)*
*Heavy-duty shears or strong knife (only for use by Mom and Dad)*
*2 pieces (10 feet each) of heavy rope*
*Lounge pad (or pillows)*

This is a modern version of the old tire swing.

Ask for an old worn tire at the tire store. The tire must have a large enough width to fit a child's body. Cut off half the tread, leaving half for a backrest and seat. Cut out two small holes to hold the rope. Tie a long piece of heavy rope to a strong tree limb and thread it through one of the small holes. Tie it off securely. Repeat for the other side. Fit a small plastic lounge pad inside the tire swing for more comfort.

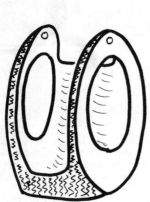

# Platform Shoes

◆

## Materials

*2 large coffee cans*
*Hammer and nail*
*Scissors*
*5 yards of rope, approximately*

If you're tired of being the shortest kid on the block, make a pair of these platform shoes.

Invert cans. Punch a hole on either side of one can with the hammer and nail, near the bottom. Tie a short piece of strong rope through the holes and knot each end so it won't come out. Tie a second piece of rope in the middle, as shown, to hold on to while walking. (Measure the length to fit.) Repeat with second can.

Hop up and start strutting, holding onto the rope lengths. Set up an obstacle course to walk over, around, on, and through. For fun, wear an old pair of Dad's pants to cover the can and ropes.

# Chalk Darts

◆

## Materials

*6 feathers (each 12 inches long)*
*(available at hobby or dime store)*
*6 wine corks*
*Sharp knife*
*Rubber cement*
*6 small pieces of chalk (3 of one color,*
*3 of another)*
*White construction paper*
*Black felt-tip pen*
*Masking tape*

These are safe darts that help develop eye-hand coordination.

Stick end of one feather into the larger end of a wine cork. With a knife, carve a small hole in other end of the cork and add a few drops of rubber cement. Insert a small piece of colored chalk and allow to dry. Repeat, making 3 darts with one color chalk and 3 with another color.

On a piece of white construction paper, draw a target with black felt-tip pen. Tape target to garage door wall and throw darts at target. Add up points to determine the winner.

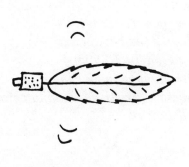

# Sand and Water Wheel

◆

## Materials

*Half-gallon milk carton*
*Scissors*
*Plastic yogurt container*
*Tagboard (or cardboard)*
*Clear Con-Tact paper*
*White glue (such as Elmer's)*
*Chopstick (or stick of similar size)*
*Small funnel*
*Small cup*

Clean out half-gallon milk carton and cut holes in 2 opposite sides, as shown. Fold in top and cut out circle to hold funnel. Cut a 1-inch ring from a plastic yogurt container. From tagboard or cardboard, cut out eight 2-by-1-inch strips. Cover with clear Con-Tact paper and fold strips in half. Glue the strips around the plastic ring as shown (A). Allow wheel to dry.

Poke a hole in either side of milk carton, as shown. Place wheel inside carton, and insert a chopstick or other wooden stick through the carton holes and the wheel.

Rest a small funnel at top of carton, being sure it does not hit wheel. (If your funnel is too long, lower the wheel.) Place a small cup in the bottom of container. Drop sand through funnel and watch it turn wheel and empty into cup at bottom.

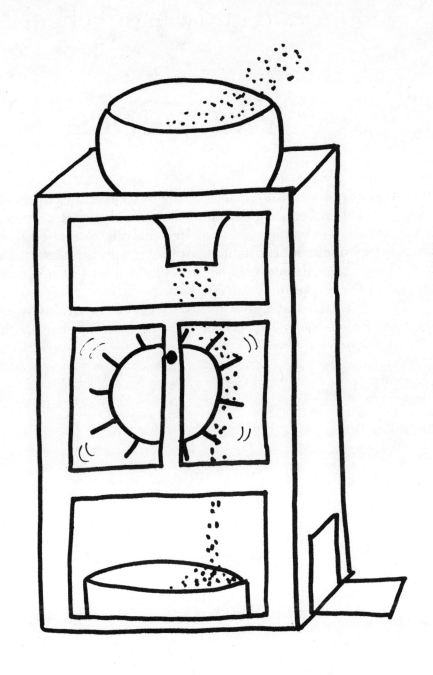

# · 9 ·

# *Water Toys*

Water is a fascinating toy in itself and can provide hours of educational play. Fill a tub with water, add a few things to squirt, fill, measure, and sift, and you'll learn about such important scientific concepts as weight, measurement, and volume. You might try a few toys from the chapter on Bath Toys, too.

The Water Toys in this chapter can be used in swimming pool, lake, ocean, and river, and even with the backyard hose.

# Gold Diggers

◆

## Materials

*Gold enamel spray paint*
*10 small rocks or stones*

So simple, yet so much fun. Spray-paint rocks with gold paint and allow to dry. Be sure to cover rocks completely.

When dry, toss them into the water and race to see who can collect the most gold nuggets. This activity encourages little ones to put their heads under water and open their eyes—good pre-swimming preparation. Older children can race for the nuggets, collect them with their eyes closed, time themselves to see how fast they can collect them, time themselves to see how many they can collect in one breath (again, good breath-holding practice).

And the gold paint helps them be seen in a pool or lake setting more easily.

# Slippery Slide

◆

## Materials

> *Old plastic sheet (or tablecloth, shower curtain, or large plastic garbage bags, cut open and taped together at the ends with plastic tape)*
> *Tent pegs (or other heavy objects)*
> *Hoze and nozzle*

Here's an inexpensive and exciting way to keep cool on a hot day.

Lay old plastic sheet, tablecloth, shower curtain, or plastic garbage bags out on the lawn. Secure the corners with tent pegs pounded into ground so ends don't stick up, or place some heavy objects on the corners (be careful not to use anything with sharp edges). Place hose nozzle on "spray" setting and set it at one end of the plastic, with the water running down the plastic. Run and slip and slide. It's even more fun when the plastic is placed on a slight incline.

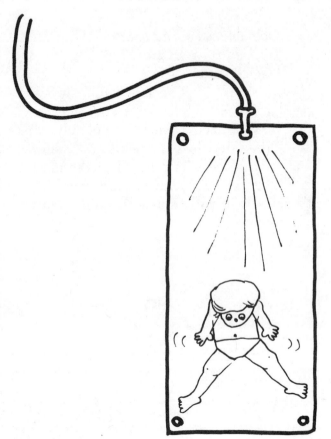

# Water Basketball

◆

## Materials

*2 wooden (or Styrofoam) rings (approximately 15 inches in diameter)*
*3 wooden dowels (each approximately ¾ inch in diameter, 18 inches long)*
*Waterproof glue*
*Foam or Nerf-type ball*

You can make this toy out of two different materials, wood or Styrofoam. If using wood, use waterproof glue to attach the 3 wooden dowels as shown, spacing them evenly around ring. If using Styrofoam, push dowels into foam, then remove them, add waterproof glue, and reinsert dowels. Let dry overnight.

Toss hoop into water and play water basketball, using a foam or Nerf-type ball. Play in teams for points or just practice making baskets.

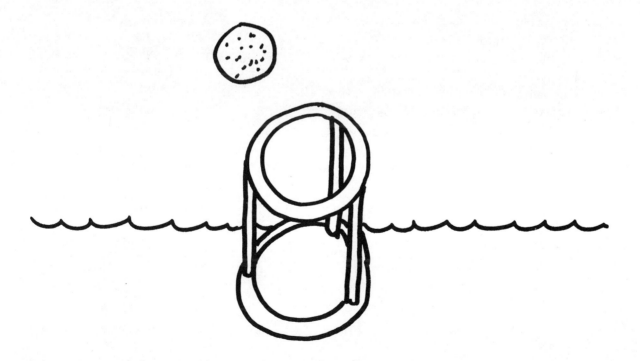

# Water Fighters

◆

## Materials

*Water balloons*
*Squirt guns*
*Sandwich baggies*
*Rubber bands (or string)*
*Food coloring*
*Tub of water*
*Old sponges*
*Plastic squirt bottles (window cleaner, etc.)*
*Turkey basters*
*Plastic catsup bottles*
*Plastic beach buckets*
*Scissors*
*Aluminum foil pans*
*String*

You don't have to have a swimming pool to have fun with water. Have a water war.

Besides the old water balloon–squirt gun methods, there are several other ways you can wage your war. Fill sandwich baggies with water and tie off the ends. Add a few drops of food coloring for special effect. Provide a tub of water with a bunch of old sponges for throwing. If you're short on water guns, use old plastic bottles that squirt. (Be sure they are thoroughly cleaned before using, and *do not use* any that contained harsh chemicals.) You can also try the turkey baster or the plastic catsup bottle. Or, if you want to do some serious water fighting, use plastic buckets to fill with water. For shields, punch holes with scissors in either end of aluminum foil pans. Tie string across for handles.

baggie

sponge

squirt
bottle

turkey
baster

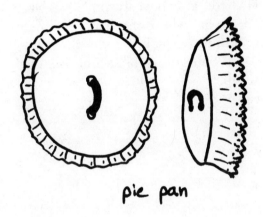

pie pan

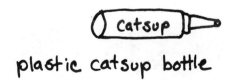

plastic catsup bottle

plastic bucket

# Sea Scope

◆

## Materials

*Scissors*
*Half-gallon milk carton*
*Plastic wrap*
*Waterproof glue*
*Clear tape*

This toy is especially fun at a lake, river, or ocean, where there are lots of interesting things to look at under the water. It can also be used in the swimming pool or bathtub.

Cut a circle from bottom of half-gallon milk carton. Stretch plastic wrap over bottom of carton to make the lens and glue it to sides as follows: Glue one side and tape down securely, then glue opposite side and tape down securely. Repeat procedure with last 2 sides, smoothing wrap out as you go. This gives you a clear lens. Open the spout of the milk carton, place the bottom in water, and look down.

# Super Tube

◆

## Materials

*Truck-size inner tube*
*Bicycle pump*
*Tire-patch kit*

*Optional:*

*Large piece of canvas*
*Awl*
*Nylon twine*

Your local tire shop has some Super Tubes (used large inner tubes) just waiting for you. They may need a patch or two, but it's certainly worth the trouble.

With a bicycle pump, inflate your gi-gantic tube. Check for holes and patch with a tire-patch kit from the local auto parts store.

Now throw "Paul Bunyon's Donut" into the nearest large lake or pool and try to stay on top.

When summer is over, this toy doubles as a mini-trampoline. Measure a piece of canvas to fit over the open hole and down the sides. Using awl, punch holes around the edges every few inches. Lace canvas closed across the bottom with nylon twine. Then turn it back over and start jumping.

# · *10* ·

# *Learning Games*

Children learn faster and enjoy it more when an educational chore is turned into a learning game. The games in this chapter can be adapted for all ages. Many can be played alone, but it's always more fun if the family can play together.

Cover all the games you make from tagboard with clear Con-Tact paper. The toy will last a long time and you can even write on the board with water-based felt-tip pens and wipe it off.

With Learning Games there will be less resistance to learning, better results, and a good time—all in one.

# Bowling

◆

## Materials

*Colorful Con-Tact paper*
*Scissors*
*10 potato-chip (or tennis-ball) cans*
*    with lids*
*Small ball*
*Sand or dried beans (optional)*

This game is adaptable to all ages. The level of skill can be determined by the distance away from the pins and the size of the ball you use.

Measure colorful Con-Tact paper to fit around can, cut, and cover each can with the paper.

To play, stand the cans up in a triangular format and roll a small ball down the floor and knock them over. You can also build them up into a pyramid shape and try to knock them down. To make the cans harder to knock down, fill with a few inches of sand or dried beans.

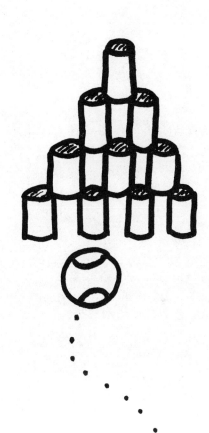

# Mouse Maze

◆

## Materials

*Wooden (or strong cardboard) box*
  *(approximately 12 × 10 inches)*
*Pencil*
*Scissors*
*Pieces of poster board in different*
  *colors*
*White glue (such as Elmer's)*
*Felt-tip pens*
*Marble*

You'll need a wooden box or strong cardboard box for this game that helps develop eye-hand coordination.

Pencil a maze design, like the one in the example here, over bottom of box. Make path twisting and intricate, leaving openings and making dead ends, but be-ing sure there is a clear path from one side of board to other. Make some covered areas, and fill in rest of board with false paths.

Cut strips of different-colored poster board the same depth as the box. Curl, bend, and fold strips as necessary and lay them out in your pattern on the board. Glue side edge of strips into place to create a three-dimensional maze. Draw a mouse hole at beginning of maze and a slice of cheese to designate the end. To make it more difficult, make designs in the paths with felt-tip pens.

Drop the marble "mouse" at the beginning "hole" and help him find his way to the "cheese" by tilting the box.

# Flannel Tale

◆

## Materials

*Children's book*
*Scissors*
*White glue (such as Elmer's)*
*Sheet of tagboard (or sides of cereal box)*
*½ yard flannel*
*Large piece of felt*
*Old cookie sheet*

Buy a favorite children's book at the dime store and cut out significant characters and props from the story. For example, if you chose *The Three Little Pigs*, cut out pigs, wolf, houses, and so on.

Glue pictures onto tagboard and the tagboard onto the flannel. Let dry, then cut out pictures (on their backing). Glue piece of felt to old cookie sheet. Propping cookie sheet at an angle so pieces will not fall off, take turns telling or acting out the story.

# Sock Box

◆

## Materials

*Scissors*
*6 quart-size milk cartons*
*6 different small objects with different textures (not sharp or harmful to child)*
*6 old socks*

This is a "feely" guessing game you can change each time you play.

Cut the tops off several quart-size milk cartons and place a different object from around the house or yard in each. Pull an old sock over the box so that the elastic is at the top, and let your child reach in, feel, and guess what's in the milk carton.

# Scratch 'n' Sniff Puzzles

◆

## Materials

*Scratch 'n' sniff stickers*
*Scissors*
*Large sheet of tagboard (or sides of cereal box)*
*Felt-tip pens*

Here's a smelly puzzle to try. In these puzzles you will match numbers and shapes. Try one with the eyes closed after a while.

Buy a package of assorted scratch 'n' sniff stickers. Cut out 2-piece jigsaw puzzles from tagboard, each one different. On one side of each puzzle place a sticker; on the other side write the number "1." On one side of the second puzzle place 2 stickers; on the other side write the number "2." Continue until you have used up the stickers.

# Gone Fishin'

◆

## Materials

*Ruler*
*Scissors*
*Tagboard (or sides of cereal box)*
*Felt-tip pen*
*Paper clips*
*Little toys, peanuts, popcorn, etc.*
*Small magnet*
*Yard-long piece of string*
*Stick (approximately 36 inches long)*
*Large box (or chair covered with*
*    sheet or towel)*

You can go fishin' for words, math problems, or just for fun, but you'll need a friend or parent to help you with the "bait."

Cut up tagboard into 3-inch squares and write out some math problems, spelling words, and so on. Attach a paper clip to each flash card that you make and attach that to a little toy, a peanut, a small bag of popcorn, and so on. Tie a small magnet to end of string; tie string to stick. Place items in the bottom of a large box or behind a chair covered with a sheet or towel. "Fish" for items without peeking. To keep your prize, you must solve the math problem, read the word, answer the question, and so on.

# Shape Puzzles

◆

## Materials

*Variety of small objects in different shapes (such as small ball, coin, ring, or shapes cut from tagboard)*
*Permanent felt-tip pen*
*8 to 10 plastic margarine tubs with lids*
*Scissors*

This game involves classification—an important skill for the young child to practice.

Outline each chosen shape with permanent felt-tip pen on the lid of a tub and cut out the shape. Replace lids on tubs. Set out objects and try to match item with shape on lid. Find as many items as you can to match the shape (small boxes or blocks for square shape, erasers or dominoes for rectangle, etc.).

# Silly Stories

◆

## Materials

*Children's book (or photographs)*
*Scissors*
*White glue (such as Elmer's)*
*Cardboard squares*
*Hole punch (or metal skewer or other*
  *sharp instrument)*
*Scraps of yarn*
*Felt-tip pen*

Sequence puzzles help children organize their thinking.

Purchase an inexpensive children's book or select a few photographs from last year's vacation. Cut out 4 or 5 pictures— or use 4 or 5 photographs—that show a sequence of events. Glue each picture to a separate cardboard square. Punch a hole at the top of each picture and attach a piece of yarn. Lay pictures out in order; pull yarn up to top and tie together. Turn the pictures over and number their order.

The object is to put the pictures together in sequence. When the choices have been completed, check other sides of pictures to see if choices were right.

An interesting variation is to arrange the pictures in any sequence and then take turns making up a story to match.

# Memory Games

◆

## Materials

*Scissors*
*2 identical books with small, clear*
 *pictures*
*Tagboard*
*White glue (such as Elmer's)*
*Clear Con-Tact paper*

With one pack of homemade cards, you can play three games that increase memory, vocabulary, and cognitive skills.

Cut out 20 to 30 small, identical pictures from your books. (The teacher supply stores have excellent books with alphabet letters and numbers corresponding to pictures that would be ideal for this activity.) Cut tagboard into several small squares; glue each picture to a separate piece of tagboard and cover with clear Con-Tact paper to preserve.

*1. Concentration.* Mix pictures and lay them face down on the table. Take turns trying to find a match.

*2. Fish.* Play Fish using your homemade cards. Each match makes a book. Whoever has the most books wins the game.

*3. What's Missing?* Set 2, 3, or 4 pictures on the table and describe each one aloud. Cover pictures with a box, then remove or turn over one. Guess which one is missing. If you do, you get to keep it.

# Brainy Bingo

◆

## Materials

*Scissors*
*Sheet of tagboard (or sides of cereal box)*
*Permanent felt-tip pen*
*Clear Con-Tact paper*
*Erasable watercolor markers*
*Beans (or other small objects)*
*Damp cloth*

Bingo can be played at any level to teach nearly anything.

Cut out several square pieces of tagboard and draw a grid in permanent felt-tip pen, allowing 4 or 5 squares across by the same amount down on each. Cover cards with clear Con-Tact paper. Cut out several dozen small cards to match the bingo cards.

With erasable watercolor markers, draw or write information on large cards, then write corresponding information on small cards. Distribute beans to each child playing and pick one small card at a time, giving children time to find match on large card. To change the game, wipe the cards with a damp cloth and rewrite another game.

## Suggestions for games:

*For younger children:*

*Color matching*
*Shape matching*
*Letter matching*
*Number matching*

*For older children:*

*Word matching*
*Upper- to lower-case alphabet*
*Math problems with answers*
*Opposites*
*Scrambled words*